James Nowlan
The Alderman and the GAA in His Time

To Teresa,

with kind regards,

Jim Walsh

First Published in Ireland 2013

———◇○◇———

Copyright © 2013 by Jim Walsh
Published by Kilkenny County Board GAA
Nowlan Park, Co. Kilkenny

Cover portrait, design & typesetting by David Nowlan

ISBN
978-1-78280-199-3

Printed in Ireland
by
dualprint
www.dualprint.ie

Acknowledgements

Composing these couple of paragraphs is probably the easiest and certainly the most pleasurable part of the project. It is indeed a pleasure to recall, for the purpose of thanking them, the many people who willingly and enthusiastically discussed the period with me and sometimes directed me to sources I might not have otherwise found.

I wish to record my thanks to the staffs of several institutional bodies which were central to my researches. In particular I wish to acknowledge the help received from Declan Macauley, and Damien Brett at Kilkenny Research Library, Mary Flood and the staff of Rothe House Library, Brian Tyrell and Phil Moylan at Kilkenny City Hall, Niabh Hennessey at Smithwick's Visitor Centre and Mark Reynolds, Archivist at the Croke Park Museum. The staffs at the National Library, the Public Records Office, the Valuation Office, the Bureau of Military History and at Glasnevin Trust, all in Dublin and also at the Public Records Office at Kew, London were ever helpful.

In all cases I encountered people who were courteous, co-operative and willing to share their extensive academic knowledge.

I wish to thank the following for the advice, information or suggestions I received from them: Denis O Reilly, Keeper of the early minute books of the Gaelic League in Kilkenny, Gerry O'Neill, Pat De Loughry, Dan McEvoy, Tommy Lanigan, Ita Bolger, Conor Denieffe, Prionsíos O'Drisceoil, all from Kilkenny, Declan Dunne, Dublin, Mairead Burke,Carrick-on-Suir, Tess Kennedy, Waterford, the late Seamus O'Brien, Dungarvan, Dan Kenny, Piltown, Willie Nolan, and Michael O'Byrne, dualprint, Dublin and Joe Dunphy, Thomastown.

I was most anxious to procure and include a photograph of the present day Nowlan Park. I am especially indebted to Eddie Hughes for the splendid image in the publication.

I acknowledge the immense contribution of my co-researcher and friend, Martin Gahan. He was involved in the project from the beginning, was always on call and acted as my advisor, my chauffer and guide, for journeys near and far.

To my wife Maura who was ever supportive and gave me a listening ear and guidance whenever I had doubts about terminology and also helped with the proof reading.

I have been privileged to get to know several members of the Nowlan family over recent months and especially David. He has been ever enthusiastic about the work and did much of the footslogging in Dublin for me. He put his considerable skills as an artist and photographer to use in the design and preparation of the document for printing, I am most grateful.

At an early stage in the project I made contact with Professor Kevin B. Nowlan who was a grand-nephew of James. Kevin was very excited at the prospect of having a biography of his famous kinsman and gave me every support and encouragement.

I am deeply grateful for his inspiration.

Unfortunately Kevin died suddenly earlier this year, aged 91 years old.

Réamhrá ó Uachtaráin Cumann Luthcleas Gael

Is cúis mhór áthais dom na focail seo a scríobh don leabhar nua seo a dhéanann mionscrudú ar shaol James Nowlan.

It gives me great pleasure to welcome the publication of this biography of James Nowlan whose contribution to the early days of the GAA was hugely significant.

The GAA is a confident well organised association respected across the island and further afield but when assessing figures such as James Nowlan and their input to its growth, it is worth casting ourselves back into the era on which they left their mark.

To say it was different would be something of an understatement.

Firstly, the GAA was a fledgling organisation still finding its way in an Ireland of far less certainty than today – even allowing for our current challenges.

Our network may have taken root but our games and their schedules had not bedded down to anything like we would consider to normal in this day and age.

To that end the vision and foresight shown by the leaders of the Association in the early years should never be underestimated.

Their vigour and drive was hugely important in stabilising the early direction of the GAA, all at a time when the nation as a whole found itself at a crossroads.

James Nowlan was one such man.

That he helped the GAA to chart a largely neutral path away from politics and the national issue as President at the turn of the last century when both were live issues is testimony to his success in putting personal views to one side for the betterment of the organisation.

Of course his name has entered modern day GAA vernacular not least because it lends itself to the home of our most successful hurling county and Nowlan Park is a venue that hosts some of our most eagerly anticipated games, not least this year's league hurling final and a memorable hurling qualifier between Kilkenny and Tipperary.

I welcome the publication of this book and its addition to the GAA library and laud the efforts involved in ensuring that an important GAA story has been captured for future generations.

Rath Dé ar an obair,

Liam Ó Néill

Liam Ó Néill
Uachtarán Chumann Lúthchleas Gael

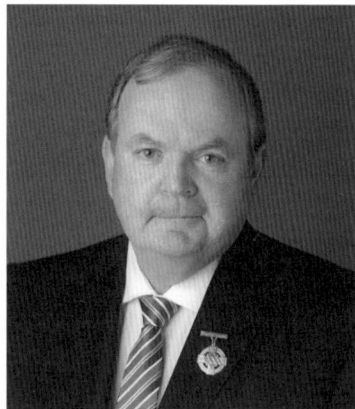

Introduction

I had been aware from an early age that James Nowlan was President of the GAA for twenty years but the significance of that length of tenure as head of the largest sporting organisation in the country only became fully appreciated in later years.

In any organisation leadership can be challenging. Leaders are expected to lead and be in control but they are also expected to smooth out and make disappear any disputes or disagreements that arise and to do so to the satisfaction of all members!

To become President or Chairperson at any level in our organisation it would be useful to have as many as possible of the following characteristics; commitment, perseverance, tolerance, patience, determination, endurance, fortitude, self-control, stoicism, in short to be well on the way to sainthood. To remain at the top for any prolonged period then requires all of the above plus politically sensitive antennae, a thick skin and family/friends who do not expect you to be the recipient of congratulations and tokens of admiration all of the time!

That James Nowlan held such a position for so long suggests he had to have been a person of exceptional talents. Such a realisation was what motivated me to examine his career, to see what depths of character motivated and enabled him to be the leader he was in a demanding period in the history of both the country and the Association.

The reader will decide to what extent the study has been successful.

Jim Walsh

James was the 6th child of Patrick Nowlan and his wife, Catherine Fitzgerald. Patrick and Catherine were married in St. Canice's Church, Kilkenny in 1852. He was a cooper by trade and was employed in Sullivan's Brewery[1] in James' St..

Kilkenny, like to the rest of the country, was then in a greatly depressed state both economically and socially, in the aftermath of the dreadful famine of the 1840s. Basset's Directory recorded that the population of the borough area declined from 19,975 to 14,174, almost 30%, from 1851 to 1861. Deniffe[2] ascribes solid economic and social causes for the origin of Fenianism:

Business crushed, industry paralysed . . . the emigrant ship, . . . the poorhouse, . . .   The excessive taxes extorted from the poor farmers and other taxpayers . . . [3]

Such was the environment in which the Nowlans started their married lives at No. 50, Patrick St. This was a less than desirable part of the city at the time in which large families lived in one or two roomed tenements or where two or more families shared sparse and depressed accommodation.

By the end of the decade there had been five children of whom one seems to have died viz. Margaret, baptized 12/12/1852, Ellenor, bap. 27/7/1854, Michael bap. 18/5/1856, Mary, bap. 25/6/1858, Mary, bap. 25/5/1860. All of the above were baptized in St. Patrick's Church and the place of residence was recorded as Patrick St. except Mary (1858) who was baptized in St. Canices and the residence was noted as Dean St.

About this time, 1860/61, the family was obliged to leave Kilkenny and set up a new home in Monasterevin, Co. Kildare. The coopers trade, in common with all industry, was in recession in Kilkenny since the 1830s[4] and Patrick was obliged to **'follow the work'** and got employment at Cassidy's Distillery in the Kildare town. They lived in the townland of Cowpasture, on the outskirts of the town at the time, and it was here that the future President of the GAA was born. James was baptized on 25/5/1862 in Monasterevin Parish Church of Sts. Peter and Paul. Two further children joined the family, John bap. 29/5/64 and Catherine bap. 5/8/1866. The family returned to Kilkenny circa 1870 and Patrick again got employment in Sullivans.

Parish Church of Sts. Peter and Paul, Monasterevin, Co. Kildare

Not surprisingly the Irish Republican Brotherhood (IRB) was strong in Kilkenny, the home town of James Stephens it's founder, and there is no doubt that Patrick Nowlan had been involved with the organisation before he went away. Little is documented in regard to his connection with the IRB. However due to the highly secretive manner in which that organisation operated this is not surprising. It was at the time of his death in 1909 that we learn of his long term connection with the organisation and its leaders from the extensive coverage provided in the National and Provincial Press. He was then variously referred to as:

The last of the '67 men', 'a close confidant of Stephens', 'his right hand man', 'an unrepentant Nationalist', 'probably the last survivor of the devoted band of Fenians in Kilkenny', etc.

His name does appear in various publications and on lists of people supporting the nationalist cause. The **'Freeman's Journal'** published a letter on May 2nd 1878, regarding the **'Released Prisoners Fund'**. The fund committee had recently collected £50 in Kilkenny and Thomastown and was thanking those who had contributed. The members of the committee were listed and included Patrick Nowlan. The financial support of the families of Fenian prisoners was a widely practiced tradition by the IRB membership.

When John Haltigan died in 1884 a fund was established to erect a memorial to his memory. It was called the Haltigan Memorial Fund. Patrick was again on the organising committee. John Haltigan was born in 1819 and grew up in Upper Patrick St. Kilkenny. He became a prominent IRB member and in 1865 was convicted of membership and was sentenced to seven years penal servitude. Having served four years he was released and went to New York. He returned to Kilkenny in 1877 and died in Cork on July 10 1884. Haltigan Terrace in Kilkenny is named in his honour.

The form of memorial chosen by the above mentioned

committee was a Celtic Cross grave monument which they had erected in St. Patrick's graveyard, Patrick St. Kilkenny. It can still be viewed there, it is the only headstone in the cemetery with a Celtic Cross and as such is easily identified. The monument bears the following inscription :

Erected to the memory of John Haltigan by the nationalists of Kilkenny who have known him to make a life long struggle for Irish freedom for which crime British law, aided by the informer Nagle, consigned him to a living tomb where the fiendish torture of years shattered his vigorous form but failed to subdue his noble spirit. May his unselfish patriotism be imitated until Ireland is once again a Nation. Died 10 July 1884 aged 66 years. R.I.P.

In subsequent years this monument became the meeting place for the Manchester Martyrs' commemorations.

On June 13th 1894 at a meeting was held in the Town Hall to make arrangements for the visit of Jeremiagh O'Donovan Rossa to Kilkenny. A large crowd was present and both Patrick Nowlan and James Nowlan were in attendance. James was at that stage obviously a fellow believer with his father of the IRB creed. The meeting became rather prolonged and James more than once admonished the chairman to get on with the business and suggested that a sub-committee representing all the clubs present should be formed to finalise the arrangements. The proposal was eventually adopted.

While Fenianism was in the main a physical force movement some of its most prominent members were motivated to achieve the revival of the Gaelic language and Gaelic games. Many of the Fenian Centres in Connacht and Munster were Irish speaking and enthusiasts for the restoration of the language in an independent Ireland[5]. It can be safely claimed that the early support achieved by the Gaelic Athletic Association after its founding in 1884 and to a lesser extent the Gaelic League when it was founded in 1893 was due in a significant measure to the IRB. The GAA was infiltrated by the IRB from the beginning and this proved highly effective both in stimulating a militant national spirit and in recruiting members for the IRB[6].

The anecdotal evidence indicates that James did not attend secondary school but joined his father as an apprentice cooper in Sullivan's at an early age. The coopers trade was "closed", i.e. the craft tended to be passed from one generation to the next. Most of Patrick's family were coopers. It was a highly skilled trade that required up to seven years apprenticeship to qualify. The above was the background in which James Nowlan grew up in Kilkenny. No doubt he accompanied his father to various gatherings where the IRB cause was championed and thus learned the history and traditions of the Irish revolutionary movement. He was later, as we shall see, to demonstrate that he had truly imbibed the philosophy of nationalism. He spent his life promoting Irish culture particularly the games and the language as well as the struggle for independence for our country.

James Stephens, founder of the Irish Republican Brotherhood, 1824 - 1901

Nowlan was 22 years old when the GAA was formed in 1884. Maurice Davin had been elected President and Michael Cusack as Secretary. From the beginning Cusack was anxious that it was not seen as a political movement, this despite the fact that he had himself in 1867 taken the IRB or Fenian oath[7]. In the light of the developing nationalist sentiment at the time and the fact that he had canvassed the support of Home Rule leaders this was an idle aspiration. Very significant also in this respect was the attendance at the inaugural meeting in Thurles of Irish Republican leaders, J. K. Bracken (Tipperary) and John Wyse Power (Waterford). Soon large numbers of IRB members had joined. Apart from their genuine interest in promoting the new association it provided them with ideal opportunities to congregate and develop their own plans without suspicion by the authorities. If that was their expectation they were mistaken.

From as early as 1887 the Royal Irish Constabulary (RIC) was infiltrating clubs and noting movements and activities of suspects[8]. Nowlan was later to be the subject of such surveillance as we shall see. The headquarters of the British police force in Ireland was at Dublin Castle.

Dublin was policed by the Dublin Metropolitan Police (DMP) while the Royal Irish Constabulary (RIC) policed the remainder of the country which had both a regional and a county structure. The officers of the RIC/DMP were the eyes and ears of the force in each village, town and parish in the country. Monthly reports were compiled by the County Inspector and forwarded to headquarters which meant that vast amounts of information were accumulated. Fortunately those reports have survived and can be accessed at the Public Records Office (PRO) London. As mentioned, from 1887 some of the GAA leaders and prominent members were deemed suspect and their movements and activities monitored and often included in the monthly reports. Cuttings from newspapers considered sympathetic to the nationalist cause were sometimes also included.

Ramón, p.75, describes the origin of the Fenian Oath as follows:

On March 17th 1858, St. Patrick's Day, Denieffe arrived in Dublin, went to Stephen's lodgings behind Lombard St., delivered money and documents, and that very day the official foundation of the new movement was effected. Luby drew up an oath under Stephen's supervision, and that evening James Stephens, Thomas Clark Luby, Joseph Denieffe, Peter Langan, Owen Considine and Garrett O'Shaughnessy, all in turn, swore to 'make Ireland an independent and democratic republic'.

Recruiting started the very next day and every recruit was administered the oath which ran along the following lines:

I, —— —— do solemnly swear, in the presence of Almighty God, that I will do my utmost, at every risk, while life lasts, to make Ireland an independent Democratic Republic; that I will yield implicit obedience, in all things not contrary to the law of God to the commands of my senior officers; and that I shall preserve inviolable secrecy regarding all the transactions of this secret society that may be confided to me. So help me God.

Joseph Denieffe, 1833 - 1910

The founding fathers of the Gaelic Athletic Association were motivated by the realisation that the traditional Irish past-times, language and culture were being submerged under the Government policy of Anglicisation. Therefore the promotion of the old games of hurling, Irish football, athletics and language was their aim and ambition. A meeting of the governing body of the Association was held in Thurles on January 17th 1885 at which rules for hurling, football, jumping, running, weight-throwing, and cycling were drawn up and adopted.

A couple of days later the Irish Cycling Association held a meeting in Dublin at which a Mr. Macredy stated that they should **'organise athletics throughout the country to squash the GAA which was of a political nature and heretofore politics and athletics had not been associated'**. On February 21st the **'Irish Amateur Athletic Association'** was formed in declared opposition to the GAA. Cusack responded in the next edition of **'United Ireland'**, a newspaper supporting Home Rule edited by William O'Brien, M.P.:

"The GAA will not interfere with those who are not hostile to national pastimes; but will use every legitimate means, similar to those enforced by similar organisations, to resist the pernicious influence of those who encourage nothing but what is foreign to the Irish people, and at which they can be beaten".

Cusack further defended the GAA in the March 14th edition of **"United Ireland"** when he wrote:

It has been stated that the founders of the GAA requested only one class of Irish leaders to patronise the Association. When, as a member of the Dublin A.C. in 1882, I proposed the Lord Mayor of Dublin with the Lord Lieutenant as patron of the club, the latter did not accept. With these facts staring Irish athletes in the face we fail to see how any thoughtful man should blame the founders of the GAA for not having again

consulted in any way those who so emphatically opposed
what is now considered so very desirable – the union of
classes of athletes. It has been urged that the GAA propose
encouraging Sunday athletics, and that such a course would
be an open violation of the Sabbath. The GAA is well
aware that in clubs in Dublin frequented by Catholics and
Protestants, skittles and rackets are played on Sundays. The
skittle-alley and the racket-court are open to rich people
but the fields of Ireland are not to be opened to the people
of Ireland the same day. This impudent absurdity will be
removed by the GAA.

The first test of the allegiance of the public came on June 17th
1885 in Kerry when both organisations arranged athletic events
in direct opposition to one another. The outcome was a clear
victory for the GAA when hundreds of athletes participated and
it was stated that 10,000 spectators attended. The competing
event was a flop. (O'Ceallaigh, p. 38)

Central Council then, at a meeting in Thurles on July 18th,
passed the following resolution:

The GAA is not a political organisation, although it is a
thoroughly national one. Our objects are, as we have already
stated, the preservation and cultivation of national past-times,
our platform is sufficiently wide for all Irishmen, and, while
we welcome assistance from every quarter, we do not stand
in need of any support from any organisation external to our
own. At a meeting of the IAAA on November 24th it was
accepted that the GAA had control of athletic events and that
an effort should be made to reach some agreement with them.
To quote again from O'Ceallaigh, **"the Freeman's Journal" made
the suggestion in a leading article that, while the independence
of both bodies should be preserved, athletes should not be
barred from competing under either laws.'**

Common ground was eventually found on this basis, and henceforth for a considerable time each body recognised the other's

rules and suspensions, and athletes competed at meetings under the auspices of both associations.

The attempt to crush the GAA had failed. It is appropriate that we should here acknowledge that both Cusack and Davin were athletes of some distinction. We know from De Burca's biography of Cusack that he played several sports, competed in many athletic meetings and promoted sporting participation for young people.

Davin grew up in a sporting family, a family with a long tradition of sporting achievements. He and his brothers had great success in a range of sporting disciplines. Three Davin brothers represented Ireland in the first international athletics meeting between Ireland and England in 1876. Three of the four Irish victories were achieved by the brothers. Weight throwing was Maurice's speciality; at the meeting referred to he won both the hammer and the 16lb shot event. Maurice won ten Irish championships between 1875 and 1879.

Michael Cusack, 1847 – 1906

After an initial great surge of support for the Association difficulties soon began to develop. As early as July 1886 Cusack was voted out as Secretary. This was a huge decision but unavoidable in the opinions of the leaders if progress was to be made. Cusack was found to be grossly inefficient in his role and was most difficult to work with[9].

During 1885/86 the IRB were strengthening their grip on the Association by having their members elected to prominent positions. Home Rulers (non-physical force) persons were becoming increasingly concerned at this development. In April 1887 Davin resigned as President. This left a huge void on the side of the moderates and the IRB were now more or less in control[10].

The 1887 Convention held in Thurles was a stormy affair and lead to the Association being badly fractured. Like most other counties Kilkenny was divided and two rival Co. Conventions were held on December 30th. However after a six week cooling off period common sense prevailed at a further Thurles Convention on January 4th 1888.

Davin was again elected President and a satisfactory peace was restored. 1888 turned out to be a year of good progress despite serious difficulties with large debts.

1889 was again a troubled year with many counties not affiliating to Central Council. In 1890 only seven counties attended the Convention in Thurles in November. The worst was yet to come however with the **'Parnell Split'** of 1891. This almost destroyed the Association. In Kilkenny the Co. Board did not function in 1891/92 and no championships were held.

In 1893 Confederation Hurling Club and Commercials Football Club, both in the City, appealed to the other clubs to enter teams in the County championship. Only Callan responded, entering both hurling and football teams. Confederation and Commercials won their respective matches and were deemed county champions.

On Monday December 30th 1894 the first of a proposed series of conventions for the re-organisations of Gaelic pastimes throughout Ireland was held in the Municipal Chambers, Town Hall,

Kilkenny, under the presidency of Mr. Joseph Purcell, T. C.
Mr. Patrick Tobin, of the Central Executive, a native of Dublin and a former Secretary of the Association, was present and addressed the meeting. He pointed out that the assocation though national in purpose was entirely non-political and with such an assurance it is incumbent on those who wish to see Irish pastimes revived to aid in every way the good work that Kilkenny has been placed in the vanguard to bring to a successful outcome. Mr T. Quinn, Confederation club, hon. sec. read letters from several districts of the county. It was pointed out that while the City was well organised much work needed to be done around the county and particularly in the southern part. The Secretary was then asked by the Chairman to read a resolution to be put to the meeting and hoped the meeting would subsequently adopt same. The resolution was as follows:

We pledge support on behalf of the Gaels of the city and county to the Central Council, Dublin and our unstinted support to the efforts to establish branches of the GAA in the respective parishes; also that a provisional county council be formed for Kilkenny.

While many of the **'old hands'** were present the emphasis from the speakers was on getting as many young members as possible involved. After a very balanced debate James Nowlan proposed:

That if the delegates from the clubs present formed themselves into a provisional committee and tried to work up the county for the next six months much could be done particularly if one good man in each parish would lead the way.

This proposal was adopted after some further discussion.

CHAPTER 6

James Nowlan was a member of the Confederation Hurling Club and acted as honorary secretary of the club for some years in the 1890s. We will now focus on what appears to be its short but significant history. The Club was based in the Dean St. or Vicar St. area of the City and had a playing field on the Freshford Road. The first reference I have found for it was in 1887 when Confederation were represented at one of the aforementioned **'rival'** Conventions – that which supported the **'Physical Force'** side, in other words the IRB brand. For the next ten years Confederation was very much to the fore in the hurling championships. In 1888 they contested the county final and were beaten by Mooncoin. In 1893 Confederation and Commercials, a football club, as stated above, renewed playing activities after **'the Split'** by organising friendly matches. They both won their respective county finals and thereby qualified to represent Kilkenny in the All-Ireland championships. They were not played until June 1894. No other county competed in Leinster so they were straight into the All-Ireland Finals. The hurling final after some considerable difficulties on the day when the chosen venue, the Ashtown Trotting Grounds, was deemed unplayable by both teams due to flooding, was played in the near-by Phoenix Park. Confederation, which had the help of some Tullaroan players, was well beaten. James Nowlan acted as a linesman on that occasion. Ryall, pps.18/19 gives a comprehensive account of this match.

In 1895 Commercials again won the football championship and went on to represent Kilkenny. They met Pierce O'Mahonys from Navan in the first match in the All-Ireland series. The match was played at Jones's Road. They were much under strength on the day and were well beaten. This match is significant in our story as it is the only occasion when we can state with certainty that James Nowlan participated as a player. He received a bad leg injury in that match and the **'Kilkenny Journal'** of December 14th reported that he had then recovered and was able to resume work.

A farcical situation occurred before the commencement of the match. Owen Roes of Drogheda, who disputed the title of champions of Meath with the O'Mahonys, lined up for the final. A meeting of Central Council held on the field settled the dispute amicably when Owen Roes withdrew on condition that the O'Mahonys, in the event of their winning the tie with Kilkenny, agree to play the Owen Roes afterwards for the Co. Meath championship. The time and place to be fixed. The O'Mahonys went on to contest the All-Ireland final and were defeated by Arravale Rovers of Tipperary on a score line – 0-4 to 0-3.

Confederation also won the county championships in 1894 and 96 and was beaten by Threecastles in 1898. Nowlan refereed that '98 final despite the fact that his own club was involved. This indicates that at this stage he had significant status in the county and had the respect of his peers. He also refereed the hurling final in 1900 when Mooncoin beat Freshford. The Confederation Club was in existence from the mid 1880s. It was not just a sporting club. It was very much a broader social club and organised classes in the Irish language and Irish music. We do not hear of the Club fielding teams again after about 1905, it seems to have been superseded by Erins Own.

James Nowlan was widely recognised as being mainly responsible for the revival of GAA activities in the county in the aftermath of the convulsions of 1887. Again after the hiatus of 1891/92 the Confederation Club, no doubt with his leadership, got matches arranged, as mentioned above, between clubs in 1893 and succeeded in getting county championships however abbreviated completed.

CHAPTER 7

As already stated James started his working life in Sullivan's brewery but we find that he has taken up employment in Smithwicks in 1890 and remained there until 1895. He then went to work in Dublin at the Guinness brewery in James' St. Perhaps this was to acquire new skills or learn new work methods as we find him back with Smithwicks again in May 1898.

On Sunday, March 20th 1896, before his departure for Dublin, James was the recipient of an address and testimonial from his fellow members in the Confederation Club. The address which was signed by Laurence Neary, President, J. Delaney, Vice-President, John McCarthy, Treasurer and E. Sweeney, Hon. Sec. spoke eloquently of James' long connection with the club and of the immense service which he rendered to the GAA in Kilkenny. The **'Kilkenny People'** informs us that the testimonial took the form of a splendid silver watch with appropriate inscription. We are also informed that James replied in feeling terms in which he made allusion to the warm place the Confederation Club held in his memory and of his wishes for its continued success.

At this time the family lived at Bishop's Hill in the City. James and sister Ellen, both of whom were unmarried, lived there with their parents. They had been at Bishop's Hill from the early 1880s. Ellen had a career as a seamstress. James represented the Confederation Club on the Co. GAA Board. While domiciled in Dublin, see above, he represented Kilkenny on Central Council, this was the first step to National prominence.

At a meeting of Central Council held at Thurles in October 1897 a letter was read from the 1798 Centenary Committee[11] stating that the GAA was being offered two places on the Committee and requesting Central Council to appoint two representatives. A very lively debate ensued as to whether it was appropriate or otherwise for the GAA to become involved. The debate revolved around whether this Committee was political or national. Nowlan and President, Frank Dineen, were the only two who spoke in favour of sending representatives. This was not surprising as both had well known republican sympathies. Nowlan strongly argued that the Committee was simply a national body and that it was incumbent on the Association to participate. It was eventually decided not to send representatives but that GAA Clubs and members could participate in the commemorations if they desired to do so.

The 1798 centenary celebrations were, from the viewpoint of the organisers, more successful than they could have ever anticipated. Torchlight processions were organised in some towns, monuments were erected to commemorate '98 battles, lectures were arranged and visits organised to cemeteries where '98 men were interred at which orations were delivered.

A wave of national enthusiasm swept the country. Thousands of GAA members took part; many clubs and some county committees actively participated and organised celebratory events.

It was evident that Nowlan and Dineen were more aware of national sentiment than their colleagues on the Central Council.

Smithwick's brewery

CHAPTER 8

The Gaelic League was formed in Dublin in 1893 with the aim of preserving Irish as a spoken language and the creation of a modern literature in Irish. Dr. Douglas Hyde, later to be the first President of Ireland, and Eoin MacNeill were amongst the group who founded the League. It was hoped to give teachers and young people knowledge of Irish through the League's many activities and summer courses. In 1898 there were 58 branches and the number had dramatically grown to 600 in 1904. The League set out from the beginning to be non-political and non-sectarian. It welcomed members from all shades of society – rural and urban, lay and clerical, Catholic and Protestant, male and female.

From the beginning the League attracted large numbers of GAA members and close links were soon established between both bodies resulting in there being a considerable overlap in membership. This meant that the GAA clubs experienced a more mixed membership than was the case previously when it was chiefly patronised by small tenant farmers and agricultural workers in the rural areas and by tradesmen and shop assistants in the towns. Now it found that its membership included a new stratum of non-manual workers – teachers, clerks, civil servants and local officials. This helped to popularise the games in middle-class areas and in many small towns the Gaelic League formed a hurling or a football club.

Over time a new type of club officer was appearing, people with skills in writing, financial matters, etc., skills which many of the older officers did not have. This was to bring the Association to a new level of management and efficiency and enabled it to be more businesslike in its operations.

Without question the most influential body of people from those early times and right up to the present have been the primary teachers. A century ago there were two teacher training colleges for the whole country namely St. Patrick's in Dublin and De La Salle in Waterford. St. Patrick's was founded in 1875 and is still thriving while De La Salle opened in 1891 and ceased to train lay teachers in 1939. Both colleges sent out graduates imbued with a very strong sense of nationalism and a great love of Gaelic games and the Irish language and contributed in a major way to putting the GAA on a solid footing in the early 1900s. De La Salle had the distinction of having seven graduates from it's Training College being elected to the highest office in the Association, namely as President. The seven were, Seán McCarthy, Robert (Bob) O'Keeffe, Pádraig MacNamee, Séamus Gardener, Dan O'Rourke, Michael Keogh and Séamus Ryan.

In county Kilkenny teachers have been to the forefront in all aspects of the Association's activities, both on the playing pitches and in the meeting rooms. A majority of our schools have become **'hurling academies'**, thanks to the enthusiasm and commitment of the teaching staffs. No doubt this situation is replicated, be it for football or hurling, throughout the country.

A branch of the Gaelic League was formed in Kilkenny in April 1897. While James Nowlan was not recorded as being present at the inaugural meeting he soon became a regular attendee and contributor at their meetings. The League promoted and organised weekly classes in the Irish language as well as classes in Irish dancing, history and folklore for the members. The Irish classes were graded according to the level of language ability held by the pupils. The **'Kilkenny People'** newspaper carried the following notice from the Branch in its edition of June 23rd 1900:

In future the classes for the teaching of Irish will be open to the public free of any charges whatsoever. The classes as heretofore will beheld at Woulfe's Arch, Parliament St. (nearly opposite the Courthouse). On Mondays and Tuesdays at 8pm the classes will for students of Parts 1 and 2 of Fr. O'Growney's simple lessons, and on Tuesdays there will be, in addition, a special class for beginners. These classes will be open free to all classes and members of all political parties. All that is necessary to become a student is simply to go to the meeting room at the hours mentioned and attend the classes. On Fridays the classes will be for students of Parts 3 and 4 of Fr. O'Growney's Simple Lessons and after the classes on each Friday there will be a

committee meeting at which the members are requested to be present. Gifts of books for the library of the Branch are earnestly requested.

The above indicates the earnestness with which the committee approached their task. We find at the AGM of the Branch in December 1899 Nowlan is being thanked for his work with the advanced classes to whom he read from books and the available journals. This indicates that he then had a good grasp of the language and since he had not been to secondary education we must conclude he had applied himself to learning the language and got encouragement to do so. No doubt his father's influence and the Nationalism of the IRB had infiltrated his young mind. In 1900 a national debate was taking place by educational interests relating to a **'Revised Programme for National Schools'** to be introduced in September of that year. In a lively debate at a League meeting in February 1900 concerning **'Irish Education and the Irish Language'** James Nowlan proposed a motion which was carried that **'Irish be placed on a level with English in the Primary School system'**. It was agreed that this motion be forwarded to the Resident Commissioner, Dr. Starkie. Unsurprisingly there is no record of a response, however perhaps a seed was sown as in 1904 bilingual programmes were permitted for Gaeltacht regions.

At the August 1900, meeting of the Branch we find the members expressing their satisfaction that one of their students had received, a highly satisfactory result in the Matriculation Examinations. The minutes record that on the proposition of Mr. James Nowlan, Vice-president, the following resolution was unanimously adopted **'that we the members of the Kilkenny Branch of the Gaelic League at this the first meeting of the session, heartily congratulate Mr. Michael J. McGrath, Parliament St., a member of this branch, on his recent success in the recent Matriculation Examination, Royal University, and more particularly on his achievement in being the only student in Ireland who obtained a first-class honour in**

Irish'. Michael Mcgrath went on to study for the priesthood and became a missionary priest being ordained for the Welsh Mission in 1908. He had a distinguished clerical career and was consecrated Archbishop of Cardiff in 1940. He died in office on February 28th 1961.

The minutes of the first decade of the Kilkenny Branch show that Nowlan attended very regularly. We often find him being thanked for the provision of furniture or materials for the classes and for assistance at various competitions that were organised. When contentious matters arose more often than not James made a proposal that took the heat out of the debate and usually it was accepted. One gets the impression that he was seen as the wise fatherly figure whose opinions were respected. At their AGMs the secretary always published the attendance records of the membership. Each year James Nowlan was near the top of the list thus indicating his commitment despite what must have been a very demanding schedule of GAA meetings.

At the inaugural meeting of the Branch on April 24th W. Cassin, T.C. stated that there were 4,000 Irish speakers in the county chiefly in the baronies of Ida, Iverk, Knocktopher and Kells. While there is no record of a branch of the League existing in the south of the county at this time it is not surprising that there was an awareness of it's work and aims as demonstrated by the following open letter which was published in the 'Kilkenny Journal' on November 14th 1903:

In order to do something practical for the Gaelic League in Kilkenny, we, the Mooncoin Hurlers, hereby challenge our old friends, the Tullaroan Hurlers, and agree to play a friendly game with them on Sunday December 6th and that the gate receipts from said meeting be handed over to the Gaelic League of Kilkenny to help them with their gallant fight for an Irish Ireland.

On behalf of the Mooncoin Hurlers — P. Fielding, J. Quinn, T. Butler, R. Morahan, R. Smyth.

CHAPTER 9

The Local Government Act of 1898 was passed in the House of Commons on August 12th. It established democratically elected county and urban councils throughout Ireland. Previously the Grand Jury System was in operation, it had been in existence in one form or another from Norman times. The members of the Grand Juries were in the main selected, not elected, and in the 19th century were generally members of the Anglo-Irish ascendancy class. The positions were honorary.

The new councils were given a three year tenure of office. They had accountability for administrative and financial matters in their areas of jurisdiction but not judicial responsibility. Under the Act the franchise was greatly extended. Heretofore only male property owners had a vote for parliamentary elections. The Act extended the franchise to male and female property owners and heads of families – male or female. National opinion was supportive of the Act. William O'Brien, journalist and author who represented Mallow in Parliament on a number of occasions, was euphoric claiming **'for the first time since the Norman invasion it places vast departments of local government in the hands of the native race'.** (O'Day, p. 186.)

One would have expected that the changes would also have created much enthusiasm and interest at a local level. Judging by the coverage in the Kilkenny papers this was certainly not the case. All I could find in the weeks leading up to the election was references to personality and political conflicts which had occurred amongst the outgoing members and speculation as to whether or not certain members would be elected. Frequently the comments, which were fully reported, were barbed, bitter and highly insulting. The recipients, on all sides, were certainly thick skinned and replied in kind or ignored the insults.

James Nowlan was nominated to contest the election and stood as an Independent Labour candidate. He had been active in public life in the City for many years apart from his involvement in the GAA and the Gaelic League.

The election was fixed for January 16th 1899. The city was

24

divided into two wards – St. Canices and St. Johns and each elected twelve members to the Corporation. James contested St. John's ward in which there were 16 candidates. He received the second highest number of votes and thus became an Alderman[12] of Kilkenny Corporation. The first three candidates elected were, John A Healy, 383 votes, James Nowlan, 359 votes and Thomas Cantwell, 358 votes. There was much rejoicing amongst the supporters of the successful candidates when the results were announced. James was carried shoulder high from the Courthouse, where the votes were counted, and up High St. accompanied by St. Patrick's Brass Band of which he was a founder member and at this time a committee member; he played the baritone in the band for many years. Bonfires blazed throughout the ward. James was now one of the **'City Fathers'.**

He was elected an Alderman of Kilkenny Corporation at each subsequent election until his retirement in 1919. He attended his last Corporation meeting on November 25th in that year. One can truly say that his contribution to local government and to the citizens of Kilkenny City was immense.

O'Brien's hopes were realised as throughout the country large numbers of nationalist figures were elected. In Kilkenny there was a 50% change of membership in the Corporation though nationalist membership remained a minority.

Years later P. J. Devlin (Devlin P. J. (Celt), Our Native Games (Dublin 1934) p. 25 – 26, paid him the following tribute which I think is appropriate to include at this stage:

Jim Nowlan was a working man, a cooper – and never sought a prouder title. He stood high in the labour councils of his native City and was elected as a toiler to an aldermanship in the Kilkenny Corporation, a position he filled until a few years before his death. He brought to the reconstruction of the Gaelic Athletic Association the healing influence of a genial nature, singleness of purpose and sound commonsense. Séamus Ua Nualláin belonged to the Fenian tradition, and had adopted it as his national gospel. He had what many of the other Fenians lacked, a wide vision and a practical sympathy

with the younger generation of Gaels who sought an intellectual as well as a virile national resurgence. He was, accordingly, to be found amongst the earliest and staunchest adherents of the Gaelic League in Kilkenny. His was the first official signature in Irish adorning the financial transactions of the Association, though it is possible that Dan Fraher of Dungarvan may have rivalled him as a pioneer in this. Through all the turmoil of the early years he held fast to the concepts of Dr. Croke and Michael Cusack.

Alderman Nowlan attended his first meeting of Kilkenny Trades Council on February 6th 1899 as a newly elected member of the Corporation. He was always solicitous for the organisation of labour and the **'Kilkenny People'** recorded a contribution he made at that meeting regarding the lack of unity in the building trades, I quote:

'It is surprising that the building trades are not more united. It is peculiar to see so many carpenters outside a society that held out so many advantages, and now at a time when contracts are to be given away, it placed him and other labour advocates in an awkward position in forwarding trade union interests; for if the carpenters and other trades in the local builder's workshops were all in societies they would have good grounds to oppose the giving of contracts to 'jobbers', and insist on the preference being given to local trade union workshops.'

I have previously indicated the extent to which the IRB infiltrated and influenced the membership of the GAA. The Nationalist members of the new Kilkenny Corporation, though not in the majority, soon exerted their influence in publicly honouring one of their **'family'**. I refer to two events which emphasises the point. At a meeting of December 2nd 1901 they voted to confer the freedom of the city on John Daly of Limerick. Daly (1845 – 1916) was an Irish Revolutionary and leading member of the IRB in Limerick. He took an active part in the abortive Fenian Rising of 1867. He was jailed for his IRB activities more than once. He was elected MP for Limerick City in 1895 as a member of the Parnellite Irish

National League. In 1899 he was elected Mayor of Limerick City and was re-elected in 1900 and 1901.

On June 3rd 1913 we find in the minutes of City Hall a motion proposed by Councillor Magennis and seconded by Councillor de Loughry and passed unanimously:

'That we learn with regret of the death of captain George S. Anthony, the manly and daring commander of the whaler 'Catalpa' which rescued the Fenian prisoners from the penal colony, Freemantle, Australia in 1876. That a copy of this expression of regret be transmitted to his relatives in New Bedford, Mass., U.S.A.'

Kilkenny City Hall

1899 was again a trying year for the Association. Notwithstanding the entry of new members from the Gaelic League as referred to previously there were significant losses of the older members who became disillusioned due to continuous disputes both at national level and within the counties. This disharmony was frequently due to disputes over financial matters and personality clashes between officers of various boards. (de Burca (1999), pps. 61 – 64)

The annual convention of the GAA for 1899 was held in July after a number of postponements. In keeping with the atmosphere in Central Council at the time the outgoing President, Michael Deering of Cork, was opposed by J.J. Keane, a young Limerick man representing the Dublin Board. Deering had been elected the previous year and the norm at the time was a three year term. On the day however Deering survived the challenge. This was a very significant meeting also for James Nowlan as he was elected Vice-President.

As the year drew to a close the Nowlan family were greatly saddened by the death of their mother Catherine, nee Fitzgerald. She died in the family home at Bishop's Hill on Tuesday November 24th, she was 72 years old. The local papers all carried details of her funeral and burial at Outrath cemetery on the outskirts of the City. Many clubs and associations sent wreaths and passed resolutions of sympathy with James, his father and family members.

Bishop's Hill, Kilkenny city

In the early days of the new year, and new century, James Nowlan was struck by a tornado. Mr. Cornelias J Kenealy, a former Town Clerk, took a case against him at Petty Sessions claiming that he was not eligible to attend meetings of the Corporation on specified dates over the previous year. The two local papers, not surprisingly, gave the case extensive coverage. While both gave identical reports of the proceedings their headlines which I reproduce did attempt to convey different impressions.

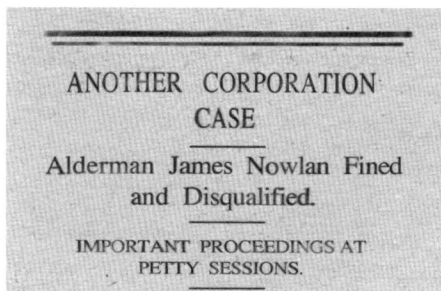

ANOTHER CORPORATION CASE	Mr. KENEALY'S ATTACK ON THE LABOUR REPRESENTATIVE.
Alderman James Nowlan Fined and Disqualified.	
IMPORTANT PROCEEDINGS AT PETTY SESSIONS.	EXTRAORDINARY DECISION A CONVICTION WITHOUT EVIDENCE
Kilkenny Journal	Kilkenny People

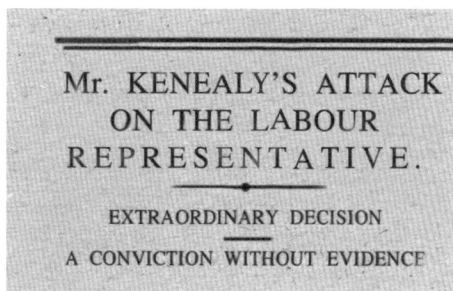

There was obviously politics at play. I reproduce the introduction to the case as outlined by the media reports on January 13th 1900:

The case of Kenealy v Nowlan was heard at City Petty sessions on Tuesday, before Mr. H. F. Considine, (in the chair) and Major P. O'Leary, J.P. It was a summons brought by Mr. C. J. Kenealy against Alderman James Nowlan under the Local Government Act, that the defendant did, on 23rd. January, 10th April, 3rd July, 4th September, 19th September, 21st November, 4th December and 27th December 1899 and January 1st 1900, at Kilkenny, in said district and city, act as a member of the Corporation of Kilkenny and of the urban district council he being at the time disqualified to so act as Councillor or Alderman, arising from the fact that he was not a Local Government elector of the Kilkenny Urban District nor a person resident in the city for twelve months previous to his election as Alderman in January 1899. There was a second summons in respect to the

8th of January 1900.'

Mr. N. Shortall, solicitor, appeared for the complainant and Mr. J. Harte, solicitor, for the defendant. The court was crowded for the hearing of the case. There was considerable legal argument between the representative solicitors, Mr. Shortall and Mr. Harte.

Witnesses were then called by both sides and cross-examined. Amongst those were Mr. Fintan Phelan, an overseer at Smithwick's brewery, Ellen Nowlan, James' sister and Mr. Frank Dineen, a former National President of the GAA and at that time its acting Secretary. Both sides then made their closing submissions and the magistrates retired to consider the evidence. After an absence of about 20 minutes they returned into court and the Chairman reported: the magistrates have made up their minds that the case has been established and that the defendant, Mr. James Nowlan, was not resident, within the meaning of the Act, during the qualifying period. With reference to the 3rd of July, 4th September, 19th September, 21st November, 27th December and 1st January, these are the seven instances, excluding the last summons, in which the penalty imposed will be 5s in each case. But the case of the 8th differs inasmuch as the attention of the defendant was called upon that occasion to the fact that he was disqualified, as we have ruled, and the fine in that case will be two guineas.

Mr. Harte – I would ask you to make the fines in the other cases large enough to admit of an appeal.

The Chairman – Then we would have to make it 21s in each case. We will do that, Mr. Harte.

Mr. Shortall – I apply for special costs

Chairman – we will give the ordinary costs, 20s in each case.

The local RIC Inspector in his monthly report to Dublin Castle for January included reference to the case and also other Corporation business:

The ex Mayor, P. J. O'Keeffe, was disqualified from his office on account of having contracts with the Corporation for printing. He was proceeded against by Mr. Kenneally, late Town Clerk, and fined. His conviction disqualifies him under the Act of Parliament for (illegible) years. E. J. Keane, O'Keeffe's lieutenant, was also disqualified as a member of the Corporation on the same grounds. The fines in each case amounted to nine guineas.

Alderman Nowlan was also disqualified as a member of the Corporation for non-residence. O'Keeffe, Keane and Nowlan are Parnellites.

James Nowlan lodged an appeal and again I quote from the local papers:

On Wednesday, June 13th 1900 at the Quarter sessions for the City of Kilkenny, His Honour County Court Judge Fitzgerald and Mr. Richard Langrishe J.P. heard an appeal by Mr James Nowlan against the decision of the magistrates at Kilkenny City Petty Sessions convicting him on a charge of acting and voting as a member of the Corporation when disqualified. The charge was brought by Mr. Cornelius J. Kenealy.

Mr. Shortal and Mr. Harte were again the representative solicitors. Mr. Harte's defence was that Mr. Shortall had not brought the case within the provisions of the Act and also that the meetings in question were irregularly called. Considerable debate on these points took place.

Mr. Shortall called some of the witnesses he had for the Petty Sessions hearing. Mr. Harte did not call witnesses but based his defence on the matters referred to above.

The judge then gave his verdict and I quote a shortened version of what appeared in the newspapers:

'A person would not be qualified to be elected unless an elector of the district or during the whole of twelve months previous to an election be a resident in the district. It is proved he had neither qualification. It is suggested he may have acted as cooper in Dublin and resided in Kilkenny. To my mind that is nonsense. You can't live 100 miles away. It appears to me that is the greatest nonsense I ever heard of. It appears to me, and my colleague agrees with me, these convictions are perfectly right. I affirm both of them with 40s costs in each case.'

This concluded the case. However the defendant was not yet prepared to concede that all was lost. The Kilkenny papers of June 30th carried the following report (this is again an edited version):

On Thursday in the Queens Bench Division before the Lord Chief Baron, Mr. Justice Andrews, and Mr. Justice Johnston the case of the Queen (Kenealy) v. Nowlan, was contested. There was considerable restating of the history of the case from either side and again the defence claiming as at Quarter Sessions that the summons was incorrectly brought to court. Finally the court quashed the conviction.

This long saga was finally over.

The Nowlans were again bereaved in June 1900 when James' brother, Michael, died. He was the eldest boy in the family and he was also a cooper. Michael and his family lived in Dublin at 4 Pyro Villas off Cork St. He and his wife, Ellen, had a family of three boys and one girl – John, Jim, Patrick and Bridget. John was the father of the late Professor Kevin B. Nowlan.

Kilkenny Court House, Kilkenny city, circa 1920s

The 1900 Convention was held in Thurles on September 9th. A decision of note at that Convention was the agreement to establish Provincial Councils. Even though provincial championships were held from as early as 1888, in one form or another, there was not a formal committee structure. The actual establishment of the Councils still took some time and it was not until November 4th 1901 that the Leinster body was formed. It was in fact the first provincial body to function. At that meeting of county representatives from Leinster James Nowlan was elected chairman and Walter Hanrahan was elected Secretary. Nowlan was to occupy that position until 1905 when he stood down, his successor was John Fitzgerald from Kildare. Walter Hanrahan (Watt.)[13] was a Wexfordman. He and Nowlan worked very well together. He remained in that post until 1916.

The Munster Council of the GAA heard the following pessimistic report on the state of the Association at the end of 1900:

The slump in the fortunes of the Association continued in the first year of the new century. A number of county boards had gone out of existence, whilst those that remained operated with a much reduced level of activity. Inefficiency at the top level of Administration was in no small way responsible for the depressing position. Personality clashes between members of the Executive resulted in needless bickering and to make matters worse much of the time of Central Council was taken up in adjudicating on a seemly endless list of trivial disputes between County Boards.

Fears were being expressed in some quarters that the Association might have to be wound up. It was obvious that the time was ripe for reform. A number of prominent officials including James Nowlan, Kilkenny, Pat Nash, Dublin, Walter Hanrahan, Wexford, and Tom Dooley lead the movement for reform. By the time the Annual Convention assembled in early September they were sufficiently organised to push through the vital decision that lead to the formation of the provincial Councils.

In his capacity as Vice-President, James chaired a special meeting of Central Council on January 20th 1901 in the absence of the President who was unavailable. He signed the minutes of the previous meeting using the Gaelic form of his name – Séumas Ua Nualláin. This was the first signature in the Irish language in the minutes of Central Council. He always signed his name in Irish whether it was on personal or business documents. This practice, when it related to official documents, was challenged by the authorities who stated they did not recognise such a signature but Nowlan never yielded to the demand to sign in the English language.

The GAA was now in its mid teenage years having had an erratic childhood – sometimes temperate, sometimes tempestuous. It now needed firm leadership to establish confidence and stability so as to enable it to prosper. Such leadership was about to be put in place.

Michael Deering, the President, died suddenly in Cork on March 25th 1901. He had been in his third year in the position. James Nowlan as Vice-President now chaired the meetings of Central Council up to the 1901 Convention on September 22nd.

The Convention was held in Thurles and ten counties were represented. Nominations were taken from the floor for all positions. Three names were nominated for the position of President – James Nowlan, M. Moynihan from Kerry and R. Cummins from Tipperary. When Moynihan and Cummins withdrew in favour of Nowlan the minutes record that Mr. Hanrahan proposed the election of Alderman Nowlan. Since there was now no other candidate he was elected unanimously.

Nominations were then taken for the position of Secretary. Again three names were proposed – Michael Cusack, Richard Blake and Luke J O'Toole. While Cusack had been voted out of office back in 1886 he had remained very active in the Dublin GAA scene. Blake had served as Secretary from 1895 to 1898. O'Toole had been born in Wicklow but had moved to Dublin at an early age. He was a successful businessman, had been a prominent player and was present as a representative of the Dublin board. When Blake's nomination was ruled out of order because he was not a registered club member the contest went to a vote between

Cusack and O'Toole. O'Toole won a close contest, the count being 19 votes to 17. The two principal positions in the Association were now filled by members who were to give an incredible 48 years service, Nowlan 20 years as President and O'Toole 28 years as Secretary.

Alderman James Nowlan 1862-1924

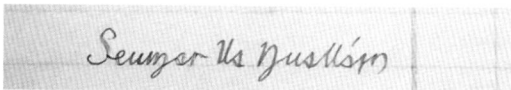

James Nowlan's signature

The 1901 Annual Convention tackled head-on a number of issues that had pestered the Association for years. Chief amongst those was its financial state. Debts had accumulated over many years and previous committees had failed to resolve the problem. We read from the minutes (p. 86) that it was agreed a sub-committee be

appointed 'to ascertain the financial position of the Association …
with a view to placing the Association on a healthy basis' and to
report to an adjourned convention later in the year. This committee
was duly appointed and was lead by Thomas F. O'Sullivan[14].

It was also resolved that a revision of the Constitution was
necessary and again a sub-committee was elected and requested to
bring recommendations to the adjourned convention. Yet another
sub-committee was elected to consider changes to the rules for hurling
and football, this committee also to report before the end of the year.

The adjourned Convention took place in Thurles on December
15th. Reporting for the **'Debts Committee'** Mr. O'Sullivan stated
that he had met Mr. M. J. Burke, Kilkenny, in Thurles on November
4th and both had investigated the debts of the Association in great
detail. A total debt of about £800 was outstanding. This included
£450 due to Michael Davitt who had contributed that amount towards
the 1888 **'America Invasion'** fund. Mr. O'Sullivan stated he was
pleased to announce to Convention that Mr. Davitt had waived his
claim and was happy to have the debt written off. (O' Toole, p. 20).

A motion was passed thanking Michael Davitt for **'his generous
and patriotic action in foregoing his claim to large sums of money
advanced by him when the Association was not in a satisfactory
financial position'** (C.C. minutes p.97). A further motion was put
and agreed that **'this convention is of opinion that a moral obligation
rests on the Gaels of Ireland to clear off all liabilities connected
with the Association since its inception.'**

We also find in the minutes from 1901 an instruction from Central
Council to the Secretary to write to all County Committees insisting
that teams competing in inter-county matches wear **'one distinctive
colour'**, and a resolution **'that no player can compete on a county
team in inter-county matches except he be a bone fide and recognised
resident of the county for which he plays'.**

The above is a sample of the issues taken on board by the new
Central Council in its first year in office.

James Stephens fell ill in his home in Blackrock, Co. Dublin on
Thursday 28th March 1901 and died at home in the early hours
of the following morning. His burial was arranged for Sunday in
Glasnevin Cemetery. The funeral procession started in Blackrock at
1pm and was accompanied by pall bearers, all '67 veterans, including

Michael Davitt. A special train was arranged to travel from Kilkenny for the funeral. It left at 9am and carried a very large contingent of mourners including the Mayor, Mr. J. Purcell, Alderman James Nowlan and several other members of the Corporation. Also on board were representatives of many of the city clubs as well as the members of St. Patrick's Juvenile Band. It was fitting that Kilkenny was well represented when one of its most prominent and colourful sons was laid to rest.

James Stephen's headstone Glasnevin Cemetery

In the early months of 1902 the minutes record the sending of delegations to Kerry, Roscommon and Mayo for the purpose of forming county committees. The new secretary also attended a number of county conventions to encourage the members to draw in new blood with a view to energising the branches/clubs in their areas.

The progress of the Association in Kilkenny was noted in the April report of the RIC to headquarters:

The GAA has been active and there has been a considerable increase in the number of clubs since last year. There are now thirty four affiliated clubs in the county, last year there was only sixteen. This has been brought about by the zeal and activity of Mr. F. P. Burke of the Inland Revenue, late Honorary Secretary resigned, Alderman James Nowlan and some others. Nowlan is a very important man. He is President of the GAA for all Ireland and is the leading IRB man in the county. A meeting of the Association was held in the Tholsel on 7th of April at which Nowlan presided. The object of the meeting was to make fixtures for the coming season, etc.. It was a stormy meeting as a number of persons came without tickets of admission and forced their way in and refused to leave; not much progress reported.

The Kilkenny county convention re-elected Joe Purcell from the Confederation club as chairman, he had been in the position since 1894 when the revival of the County Board took place. The convention elected Danny O'Connell as Secretary. Danny had a long innings as a central figure in GAA circles in the county. He was secretary 1902 – 1913 and again in 1932; he had an involvement with the senior county team selection committee and management on and off right up to 1946. He was an uncle of the famous Kilkenny goal keeper of the 1930s, Jimmy O'Connell.

On July 22nd the Archbishop of Cashel and Emly Most Rev. Dr. Croke died. Dr. Croke had been patron of the Association from its formation in 1884 and had been one of its most enthusiastic supporters. His letter of acceptance in response to Michael Cusack's invitation to become patron came to be known as **'The Charter of the G.A.A.'**

All matches and activities arranged for the following Sunday were cancelled by Central Council as a mark of respect. Many hundreds of GAA members lead by President Nowlan and Secretary O'Toole attended his funeral in Thurles on 26th.

At a meeting of Central Council later that day the following resolution was passed:

We the Central Council of the Gaelic Athletic Association desire on behalf of the Gaels of Ireland to place on record our appreciation of the irreparable loss the cause of native customs has sustained in the death of His Grace.

A similar resolution was passed at the 1902 Annual Convention. At a meeting of Kilkenny Corporation on July 29th the following motion was proposed by Alderman James Nowlan and seconded by Mr. King:

'That we express our deep and sincere regret at the demise of our esteemed and renowned countryman , the Most Rev. Dr. Croke, whose presence and eloquence were frequently appreciated by the people of Kilkenny when he came in his health and vigour on many occasions on our public platforms to sustain the national cause'.

The 1902 Convention also agreed to appoint Dr. Fennelly, Archbishop of Cashel and Emly, and Dr. Douglas Hyde as patrons of the Association.

CHAPTER 14

Central council was very active throughout 1902 and 1903. Apart from the ordinary administrative workload involved in running the Association the minutes indicate the hectic programme of innovation taken on board. Both personal and written contacts were made with representatives of clubs and counties throughout the country with the aim of establishing or furthering the playing of Gaelic games particularly in areas where they had not yet become popular. Contacts were also made in England, Scotland and America for the purpose of having provincial Councils established. Resulting from the 1901 Convention a proposal was brought to Central Council recommending a radical restructuring of the Council. This proposal was rejected.

The 1902 Convention was adjourned and at the reconvened meeting on January 11th 1903 the following matters were debated and decisions taken:

The introduction of parish rule was agreed – each county having the option of applying the rule.
it was agreed to revise playing rules triennially instead of annually, – 'as alterations to the rules year after year is calculated to confuse players and leads to endless discussions at Congress.'

The 1903 Convention was held on November 8th and was adjourned before all business was complete. At the reconvened meeting on December 13th the following decisions were made:

The introduction of a Junior All-Ireland championship was agreed, a sub-committee was formed to streamline the rules of the Association, 'the existing format was deemed to be unsatisfactory and unsuitable for reference purposes,' the price of the Official guide was reduced from 6p to 2p, so as to bring the price within the reach of every Gael, and that they be printed in the vernacular as a means of encouraging the study of our national language amongst the members of the GAA, that for association business that Kings County be substituted with the original name of Offaly; Queensboro to be referred to as Leix and Wexford to be referred to as Loch Gorman.

The meeting also made a very significant decision in relation to athletics. It was proposed and agreed that **'a sub-committee be appointed from the members of Central Council to act as an Athletics Committee and take charge of Athletics in general.'**

G. A. A.

HELP THE PRISONERS

BY ATTENDING THE

Great Hurling Contest
TIPPERARY v. DUBLIN

AT

CROKE PARK

ON

Sunday next, April 27

IN AID OF

The Republican Prisoners' Dependents' Fund

SPLENDID HURLING ASSURED
SEVERAL BANDS WILL ATTEND

Match at 3.30

Arthur Griffith, Eamon De Valera, Dublin Lord Mayor Laurence O'Neill and Michael Collins seated at a G.A.A. match in Croke Park, circa 1919

41

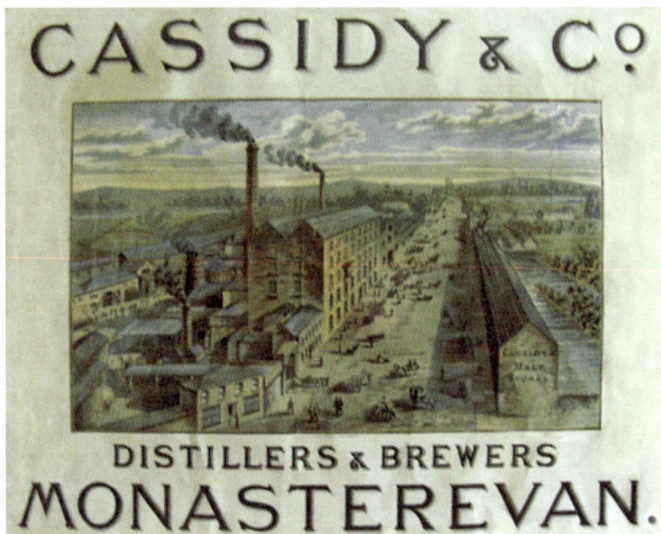

Patrick Nowlan, James' father worked at Cassidys

Professor Kevin B. Nowlan with Jim Walsh at the grave
of Alderman James Nowlan, Kevin B's grand uncle - April 2012

The unveiling of the Alderman James Nowlan headstone by Liam O'Neill GAA president, with other GAA members and some of the Nowlan clan

Kilkenny Volunteers

Back row; l to r, J. Lawlor, D. Barry, P. Corcoran, J. Nowlan, L. Walsh, T. Treacy, J. Harte, P. Brett.

2nd row; l to r, P. Parsons, T. Furlong, M. Kealy, M. Higgins, B. Denn, T. Neary, J. Lawlor, P. Purcell, P. DeLoughry,

3rd row; l to r, C. Smith, S. O'Dwyer, N. Comerford, T. Mullally, P. Burke, J. Carrigan, L. DeLoughry, S. Gibbons.

Front row; l to r, M. Ryan, J. Coyne, J. Madigan, B. Stephens.

This picture was taken after these men returned having served imprisonment in various Irish and British jails in 1916 and is on permanent display in the museum of Kilkenny Military Barracks.

A Black and Tan on duty in Dublin:
he has a Lewis machine gun

Harry Bolland smiling, Michael Collins shaking hands with Alderman James Nowlan - Croke Park 1921

Mount Brown or McCaffery Estate Dublin where James Nowlan lived the last number of years

Douglas Hyde, 1860 - 1949

Eoin McNeill, 1867 - 1945

Jeremiah O'Donovan Rossa (1831 – 1915) burial

Croke Park 1924 (Aonach Tailteann programme 1924)

CHAPTER 15

A landmark decision was taken by Central Council at their meeting on January 3rd 1904. It was decided to rent office accommodation in Dublin city centre at 68 Upper O'Connell St.[15] from which the business of the Association would be carried out. The Association was now twenty years in existence and amazingly the work of the secretary was still conducted from his home. Since his appointment Luke O'Toole worked from his residence at 29 Mount Pleasant, Ranelagh. Having its headquarter offices in the principal street of the capital city was a significant step in branding the association as a business like and national organisation; further evidence that the Association was on the move.

The strong new leadership was now getting a firm grip on all activities of the GAA and major reorganisation and expansion was evident for all to see. This progress was recognised by the editors of **'The Bold Shelmaliers'** the history of the Shelmalier GAA Club in Wexford. Dealing with the year 1905, apart from local matters, they wrote:

The influence of the national presidency of Jim Nowlan and his general secretary, Luke O'Toole, was now very evident with the enormous rise in the numbers playing the games. They had set about clearing the massive debt which the Association had incurred, a task that would take another five years to complete. They had also restored its nationalistic identity and support, which lead to the re-introduction at the annual Congress in January of the foreign games and persons ban. Other factors improved were the standardisation of the playing rules, establishment of camogie and the proper administration of county committees and clubs.

A long running dispute between the GAA and the IAAA resulted in the GAA breaking off all co-operation with the rival body in 1906. In the succeeding few years athletics was in a very healthy state in the country but thereafter tensions began to develop due to disagreements about lack of democracy in the Athletics Council in relation to decision making.

At the 1911 Congress a motion was proposed to disband the Athletics Council but it was defeated. By 1912 however a split developed in the GAA relating to the control of athletics and the demands of athletes themselves to have an input into decision making; this lead to splinter groups being formed and athletic management was in disarray. In 1913 Congress agreed to a new scheme for the control and management of athletics after which a reconstructed Athletics Council was put in place.

The next major change relating to athletics was the formation of the National Athletics and Cycling Association (N.A.C.A.) in 1922 which body was to be independent of the GAA. Central Council promised however to support the new Association in any way it could.

Peter De Loughry, Mayor of Kilkenny City

The 1901 Census of Ireland took place on Sunday night March 31st. The Nowlan household form confirms that the family then lived at Troy's Gate East in St. John's Ward in St. Canice's Parish and was signed by Patrick as head of the family. As expected it recorded that Ellen and James resided there. Also listed as residents on that night was John Nowlan aged 10 described as a grandson, and Michael Ryan aged 5 described as a grandnephew. John was a son of James' brother Michael who had died the previous year as we have seen. Michael Ryan was the son of one of Patrick siblings. We learn from oral family history that the family agreed to take young John to live with them so as to lighten the burden on his widowed mother. It is likely that Michael Ryan, John's cousin, was invited to join the family also as a support and playmate for John. At the time such a family arrangement was not uncommon as extended families often willingly supported one another in times of difficulty. It must however be acknowledged as having been a very generous and Christian act.

When the 1911 Census came round much has changed in the household. While they still live at the same address only Ellen, James and Michael Ryan are listed on the form. Patrick has died and presumably John has returned to Dublin, he was now a young man of 20 years.

Other documents have given the address as Bishop's Hill and this is the name Kilkenny people use. Their residence was one of a small terrace of 9 houses which still remain on the left hand side on Bishop's Hill as one is leaving town.

CHAPTER 17

At the 1903 AGM of the Gaelic League Branch Tomás McDonagh[16] as acting Secretary gave the annual report and expressed disappointment that two members had failed to honour an agreement by branch members that all members should endeavour to **'secure the election to public positions of candidates interested or pledged to the movement'**. Since this incident involved two national figures debating a point of principle I will now quote directly from the minutes:

Mr. McDonagh - 'Of course I refer to Alderman Nowlan and Mr. E McSweney's voting against Mr. Kennedy at a recent election. With the merits of the matter outside the Gaelic League I have nothing to do, and you will believe me when I say that if the case was reversed and Mr. Kennedy voted against Ald. Nowlan and Mr. McSweeney I would bring it before you too. I think that since the action was public, whatever explanation there is should also be made public. Personally it is painful for me to mention the matter as I have been a friend of the three gentlemen referred to, but the prestige of the Gaelic League is affected, and I do not believe I would be doing my duty in remaining silent.

The adoption of the Secretary's report was proposed and seconded.

Again I quote from the minutes:

Alderman Nowlan – Before you put the proposition – with reference to the last portion of the report – I think the secretary had a right to inform me that he was to put in such a thing. I did not come prepared to make my answer. I know Mr. O'Keeffe for the most portion of my life and I know him to be a thorough Irishman and in sympathy with every national movement; and I promised him my vote and I would break it for no man, Gaelic Leaguer or anyone else.

Mr. McDonagh said he hoped that Alderman Nowlan under-
stood that he bore him no ill-will. It was very painful of him
to have to refer to the matter.

Ald. Nowlan – I say you had a right to tell me.

Mr. McDonagh – anything that occurs with reference to the
Gaelic League Branch can come up here.

The motion was adopted nem. con. McDonagh did not allow
his name to go forward for re-election to the committee.

Tomás McDonagh, 1878 - 1916

CHAPTER 18

Kilkenny Corporation members became very animated in April 1904 when the news of the proposed Royal visit to the city became known. King Edward V11 and Queen Alexandria were on a private visit to Ireland and it was arranged that they would be guests of Lord and Lady Ormonde at Kilkenny Castle from Saturday, April 30th to Monday May 2nd. At the monthly meeting of the Corporation on Monday 4th, a motion was put by Councillor James Holahan as follows:

'I hereby give notice that I will propose that at the next quarterly meeting of the Kilkenny Urban District Council that an address of welcome be presented to His Majesty the King and Queen Alexandria on their arrival amongst us on Saturday April 30th, and that a committee is appointed to draft same.'

A large crowd had assembled at the back of the hall, mainly nationalist minded people, and they were not slow to express their views and their feelings; hence Mr. Holohan had extreme difficulty in being heard when he attempted to put the motion. After some considerable bitter and sarcastic remarks were exchanged and when the motion had got a seconder Alderman Jim Nowlan stated:

Before the proceedings go any further I wish to ask if there is any resolution with reference to the King of England by this Corporation in reference to the oath taken by him and I would wish to have it read. We can then see exactly what our position is.

The Town Clerk asked if the resolution referred to dealing with the Coronation oath. On being told it was, the Clerk then read the following resolution adopted by the Corporation at their quarterly meeting on March 4th 1901:

Proposed by Mr. O'Connell and seconded by Mr. Lennon and passed, - 'that we the members of the Kilkenny Corporation take this opportunity of placing on record our utter indignation and detestation at the outrageous insult offered to us as Catholics by the abominable and insulting language put into the mouth of King Edward V11th on the occasion of his taking of the Coronation Oath, whereby he declares that some of the most sacred dogmas of our faith to be idolatrous and superstitious.........

Alderman Nowlan:

In reference to that resolution I don't think that we, as representing the Catholics of this City in any case, would be doing our duty in having an address to a man who took that blasphemous oath.

This statement was received with loud applause by the demonstrators. After further acrimonious debate Mr. Holohan's motion was put to a vote and carried by 12 votes to 7. The reader will remember that in 1901 a motion had been passed by the Corporation to confer the freedom of the city of Kilkenny on Mayor John Daly from Limerick. This event had not taken place in the interim and Mr. Maginnis now proposed that the conferring ceremony should take place on April 30th. Alderman Purcell seconded the proposal and it was passed unanimously to the great joy of the audience who began to sing 'a Nation Once Again.'

At the Corporation meeting on April 11th a letter was read from John Daly stating he would be delighted to attend on April 30th. However a motion was put, on the requisition of 11 members, 'that the Corporation should meet on the following Monday to rescind the resolution already passed re the invitation to John Daly.' The motion was carried after further spirited debate. The meeting duly took place on Monday the 18th to consider the motion re the John Daly invitation. At this meeting further rancorous debate lead to the motion to rescind the invitation being carried and so the invitation was deferred to a later date.

The 'Kilkenny People' of the 30th printed the programme for the Royal visit. I include part of it because of some significant events, relevant to our story, that allegedly took place over the weekend and subsequently. The Royal entourage were due to arrive at Kilkenny rail station at 1.17pm. Having been received by the Marquis and Marchioness of Ormonde and by Sir William Blundon, Bart., High Sheriff of County Kilkenny they receive addresses of welcome from Kilkenny Corporation and other bodies. They then drive to Kilkenny Castle and later in the afternoon will attend the Spring Show of Kilkenny Agricultural Society at St. James' Park. On Sunday they attend service at St. Canice's Cathedral and on Monday will depart for Waterford at 12 noon. On the Saturday 14 members of the Corporation, including the Town Clerk, were present at the station for the address of welcome. The address on behalf of the Corporation was read by Mr. Edward O'Connell. The Mayor, Mr. Edward O'Shea did not attend nor did the other nationalist members.

I now include two incidents relating to the event which have survived in the Nowlan family oral tradition and were related to me by the late Kevin B Nowlan. On the Sunday the Royal party travelled from the Castle to the Cathedral by horse drawn closed carriage. The story is that James Nowlan had arranged that a group of boys would convey buckets of water to the precincts of the Cathedral and as the carriage was leaving for the return journey the boys would pour the water on the cobble stones in the street in the hope that the horses would slip or fall and thus embarrass the organisers!! This from the President of the GAA!!

It is further related that in one of the days subsequent to the visit Patrick Nowlan met the Town Clerk in the street and assaulted him by catching him by the lapels of his coat and pushed him against the nearest wall threatening him for his actions in reading the address of welcome for the Royals!

Meanwhile in Waterford a very large gathering of citizens met at the Town Hall on Sunday, May 21st, to protest against the presentation of royal addresses to the King and Queen of England on the occasion of their planned visit to the City. A resolution of protest was passed with acclamation.

CHAPTER 19

The 1904 Convention, held in January 1905, was noteworthy for its passing of the 'ban' rule which the older ones amongst us will have been very familiar with. The rule was strongly advocated and supported by President Nowlan and other prominent council members. The wording of the resolution was as follows:

That persons who play rugby, soccer, hockey, cricket or other imported games shall be suspended for two years from the date of playing such games and this rule to take effect from 1st February 1905.

It must be remembered that **'bans'** were not uncommon in the early years of the Association. The very basis on which the GAA was founded was to preserve Gaelic sports and culture. In 1885 a ban was introduced relating to athletics which was then an important part of GAA activities. Cusack resented the fact that athletics were mainly the preserve of **'an elitist faction'** which was anti-nationalist and whose aim was to destroy native pastimes. The intention was to prevent GAA members from supporting a rival athletics body and to prevent members of such rival bodies from participating in GAA athletics meetings. This 'ban' was reversed early on due to the intercession of Dr. Croke. Also in 1885 a **'foreign games ban'** was introduced on a voluntary basis as was a police boycott. The latter was deemed necessary because of the activity of the RIC members during the Land War; this was withdrawn in the 1890s.

Now in 1905 the **'foreign games ban'** was made obligatory. It was not the unanimous choice of Congress, the Cork delegation opposed the proposal but it was strongly supported and passed with a clear majority. Three reasons were put forward to justify the rule:

i   **to protect Gaelic games from competition from rival codes,**

ii   **to ensure members total loyalty to Gaelic games,**

iii   **to ensure that the police could not, by infiltrating the GAA, find out too much about the nationalistic activities of members. (de Burca, Gaelic Games, part 6, 1984)**

As we shall see the RIC still managed to gain knowledge of the movements of members and indeed of decisions taken at meetings of the national executive. The **'ban'** rule remained in the Rule Book until it was rescinded at Congress in 1971. During the many years of its existence it proved very controversial and frequently gave rise to prolonged and animated debates at meetings of clubs, county boards and at congresses. Its demise was greeted with sighs of relief in many quarters.

Kilkenny won the All-Ireland senior hurling championship of 1904. Having been beaten in the final on four occasions previously this was a significant victory, the first of an amazing run of success which resulted in the winning of seven All-Irelands in the years 1904 – 1913. The names and feats of those great teams are well documented, particularly by Ryall.

Royal Irish Constabulary

CHAPTER 20

---o---

I now include extracts from the RIC reports for the year 1908, which will give the reader a flavour of the operations of the police force at the time. The cover page for each month is headed:

Secret Societies

Precis: the month in question, e. g. January.

16th January 1908
Suspect Seamus McManus
Chief Commr., D.M.P. informs Inspector General, RIC that the above named arrived here on 9th inst. and put up at the Ormond Hotel, Gardener's Place. Next day he visited the Office of the 'Sinn Fein' newspaper 17 Fownes St., where he had an interview with Arthur Griffith, W. J. Ryan, and W. O'Leary Curtis. This meeting is said to have been in connection with the contemplated starting of a daily newspaper to be run in the interests of the Sinn Fein League and National Council Organisation. McManus left here on 11th inst. en route to Strabane.

14th February 1908
Suspect Andrew O'Byrne
Chief Commr. , DMP informs Inspector General, RIC that the above left Amien St. for Belfast on morning of 14th inst.

17th February 1908
Suspects J. Mulroy, J. Etchingham and H. Keogh
Chief Commr., DMP informs inspector General RIC that the above left Amien St. on morning of 15th inst. for Enniskillen. The object of their visit is believed to be in connection with the North Leitrim Election, they being supporters of the Sinn Fein candidate C.J. Dolan.

21st May 1908
Suspect Alderman J. Nowlan

Chief Commr., DMP informs Inspector General RIC that the above named duly arrived on 16th inst. and attended a meeting of the Leinster Council GAA on 17th. inst.

6th July 1908
Suspects Dan McCarthy and M.F. Crowe
Chief Commr., DMP informs Inspector General RIC that the above named suspects in company with L.J. O'Toole and other members of the GAA left Kingsbridge on evening of 4th inst. en route to Tipperary.

7th July 1908
Alderman Nowlan, Kilkenny
Chief Commr., DMP informs Inspector General RIC that the above named attended a meeting of the Central Council GAA in Dublin on 28th ult., and that the Council approved an application from the Wolfe Tone Committee in reference to the holding of a tournament in aid of the funds.

1st August 1908
Suspect M.F. Crowe
Chief Commr., DMP informs Inspector General RIC regarding Crowe's visit to London, that he was again observed here on 21st ult. on which date he attended a meet of the Co. Dublin Committee, GAA at 68 Upper Sackville St.

6th August 1908
Gaelic Excursion from Sligo
Chief Commr., DMP informs Inspector General RIC that about 300 persons arrived at Broadstone from Sligo on morning of 2nd inst. and returned on evening of same date. There did not appear to be any political object in their visit, and during their stay they were not observed to associate with any of the Dublin suspects.

6th August 1908
Suspect Alderman Nowlan, Kilkenny

Chief Commr., DMP informs Inspector general RIC that the above named who arrived here on 1st inst. from Kilkenny left the Kingsbridge Terminus on morning of 3rd en route to Athlone, in the meantime he attended a meeting of the Leinster Council GAA, which was summoned specially to consider the action of the Irish American Athletes in attending sports at Ballsbridge under the auspices of the I.A.A.A.

24th September 1908
Suspects Alderman Nowlan and P. Nash, Kilkenny
Chief Commr., DMP informs Inspector General RIC that Alderman Nowlan arrived here on 20th inst. and attended a meeting of Central Council of the GAA and returned home on evening of same date. Patrick Nash was not observed to accompany him on this occasion.

8th October 1908
Alderman James Nowlan, Kilkenny
Chief Commr., DMP informs Inspector General RIC that the above named was not observed to arrive here on 3rd inst. but was picked up the following day. His business on this occasion was to attend a meeting of Central Council GAA at 38(sic) Sackville St. on 4th inst. at which he presided, and returned home on evening of same date.

23rd October 1908
Alderman Nowlan, Kilkenny
Chief Commr., DMP informs Inspector General RIC that the above named arrived here on 17th inst. and returned home the next day. During his visit he attended a meeting of the Central Council of the GAA on 18th inst..

29th October 1908
Mrs. Maud Gonne McBride
Chief Commr., DMP informs Inspector General RIC that the above named arrived here in due course on 14th inst., and remained until 27th inst. when she left by Express Boat from North Wall for Hollyhead. During her stay she was not observed to associate with any suspects here, but was much in the company of Mr. W.B. Yeates at the Abbey Theatre.

30th October 1908

Alderman Nowlan and others visit Dublin

Chief Commr., DMP informs Inspector General RIC that the above named accompanied by some 200 persons from Kilkenny arrived at Kingsbridge by train indicated on morning of 25th inst., and proceeded to Jones' Road, where hurling and football contests took place between Kilkenny and Wexford. Nowlan subsequently attended a meeting of the Central Council GAA and returned home on evening of same date.

5th November 1908

Suspect Alderman Nowlan, Kilkenny

Chief Commr., DMP informs Inspector General RIC that the above named arrived here on morning of 1st inst. and returned to Kilkenny on night of same date. During his visit he attended the Gaelic football contests at Jones' Road.

27th November 1908

Alderman Nowlan, Kilkenny

Chief Commr., DMP informs Inspector General RIC that the above named arrived here by train on evening of 21st inst. He was present at Jones' Road next day, and with suspects M.F. Crowe and Dan McCarthy, assisted in superintending the arrangements in connection with the GAA contests held there. He subsequently attended a meeting of the Central Council GAA and returned to Kilkenny on evening of 23rd inst..

21st December 1908

John O'Mahony

Chief Commr. DMP in replying to a query of Inspector General RIC as to whether O'Mahony is regarded as important, states that he is agent for the Express Advertising Company, 18 Lr. Ormond Quay; that he originally came from Thomastown, Co. Kilkenny, where his mother and sister are engaged in dressmaking business; that he has been occasionally seen associating with the Sinn Fein Party, but he is not regarded as much political importance, and is seldom found attending any of their meetings.

CHAPTER 21

Kilkenny won the county's third All-Ireland in 1908. It was the final of the 1907 championship, Cork being the opposition, and was played in Dungarvan on June 21st before a reported 15,000 spectators. Once again Ryall gives a detailed account of how the flow and ebb of the scoring, with Kilkenny winning by a single point. The 1932 GAA Annual reprinted an article written some years previously by **'Carbery'**[17], in his own colourful style, describing the scene in Dungarvan on the occasion of that match:

A bright mid-summer's day in 1908 and the old borough of Dungarvan is packed to overflowing with cheerful, joyous, happy crowds of Gaels. The liquid accents of the Decies flow in sweet harmony across the salt-laden air. Thousands of stalwart Kilkennymen have come across the gentle fair river since early morn. They sport their familiar black and amber colours. Western trains puff in, out on to the tracks and on to the green fields sweep towering Corkmen with their charming accented cadence, bubbling with good cheer and confidence. Soon the streams blend in one dark human river which sought its 'bed' in Dan Fraher's spacious enclosure. Music and sunshine – sunshine and music; merry jest and ready repartee. Fr. Dollard (Slievenamon) home from America to cheer his loved Mooncoin; Pat McGrath and Alderman Jim Nowlan, with willing workers, keeping the surging crowds in control. What a day for memory to feast on, and what a game!

CHAPTER 22

The 1909 Convention took place on February 28th. The venue was the Mansion House in Dublin, heretofore Convention was held in Thurles. James Nowlan was unable to be present due to illness but was re-elected unanimously as was Luke O Toole as Secretary. Despite 1909 being the 25th anniversary of the formation of the Association the minutes do not record any reference to the fact. During the first 25 years many notable successes were achieved despite several serious reverses, particularly in the early years. De Burca, pps. 75-81 outlines the significance of the achievements and their influence on the social, cultural and sporting lives of the majority of the population both rural and urban. He further proposes that the leaders were more focussed on the future rather than the past and that to them it was more important that all their energies should be channelled into further improving all aspects of the Associations activities.

For some years after the death of Dr. Croke in 1902 Central Council had decided to establish a suitable memorial for its first and most esteemed Patron. The 1905 Convention passed the following resolution, **'that the Gaels of Ireland do erect a memorial, or some token, to the memory of the late Dr. Croke, Patron of the GAA'**. At the quarterly meeting of Central Council on March 31st 1907 it was decided to draft a circular on the memorial project and a sub-committee was appointed for this purpose.

The October meeting pledged £100 to the memorial fund and another sub-committee was appointed to **'carry the matter into effect'**. Subsequently the minutes show that the matter arose regularly at the meetings when funds and fundraising were discussed, however progress was slow.

A special meeting of Central Council was held on 17th May 1911 for the purpose of making arrangements and fixing expenses **'in connection with the homecoming of the Irish American hurling team'**. It was agreed that 25% of the profits from the match takings would go to the Croke Memorial Fund. The Irish American team was drawn from the Chicago and New York clubs. Six matches were played. The first was against the then All-Ireland champions, Wexford, which ended in a draw. Next was a match versus Tipperary when the exiles were beaten as they were when they played Kilkenny. This match was played at Waterford and attracted 8,000 spectators. The fourth match was against Dublin and was played at Jones' Road and was won by Dublin. A member of the Dublin team on the day was Harry Boland who was later to become Chairman of the Dublin Board and a prominent political figure. Particulars of the other matches appear not to be available.

The matches were well attended and resulted in big gate receipts. The expenses in connection with the tour were very high and were all covered. A grant was made to the visiting team for promotional work back in America and £104-1s-6d was lodged to the Memorial Fund.

Dr. Croke, Patron of the GAA, 1824 - 1902

1910 was a year of expansion and development for the Association. However the President had to deal with two divisive issues which had been a source of controversy for some time; a dispute relating to the Railway Shield Competition and the Waterford dispute relating to 'the playing of foreign games on Gaelic fields'. The latter issue was coming to the fore in a number of counties but it had become very inflamed in Waterford. At the National Convention, now referred to as Congress, held in the Mansion House, Dublin, on Easter Sunday considerable time was given to the matter in what became a heated debate. Mr J. J. Walsh, Chairman of the Cork Board, would not accept the word of the Waterford delegates that an agreement was imminent and eventually the Chairman ruled him out of order and demanded that he resume his seat. (O'Neill, Phil, p. 17). The matter however seems to have rumbled on for another year as we read that at a meeting of the Waterford Sportsfield Company Ltd. on April 23rd 1911 the following resolution was passed and sent to the Central, Leinster and Munster Councils:

That the Directors from this date, in the best interests of the Company refuse the use of the grounds for all sports and practices, except those that conform to the rules of the GAA.

Meanwhile the **'Kilkenny Journal'** of Saturday, February 25th 1911, had the following comment:

That the motto of "Gaelic fields for Gaelic players' is winning all along the line, and Jones' Road has followed the lead of Dungarvan, Cork, Thurles and the other places that can distinguish the difference between a hawk and a handsaw" !

The Railway Shield[18] dispute had also been contentious for some time. The Great Southern Railway Company presented two shields in 1905 for inter-provincial competitions in hurling and football. The understanding was that the Shield would be won outright by the province winning it twice in succession or by winning it three times.

The provincial champions had the right to select the team. Kilkenny (Leinster) were winners in 1905. They beat Munster to win the first match on August 20th, and on November 11th they beat Galway in the final – 4-10 to 4-05. Tipperary won in 1906 by beating Galway in the final, 9-14 to 1-05. In 1907 Leinster selected beat Tipperary, 0-14 to 1-08 in the final played at Jones' Road on 29-9-1907.

Leinster (Kilkenny) was again victorious in 1908. Before an estimated 20,000 spectators in St. James' Park on July 19th 1908 they again beat Munster (Tipperary), 0-14 to 2-05. Kilkenny now claimed the Shield. The Leinster Council however viewed the matter differently. At a meeting on St. Patrick's Day 1909, the Chairman, Mr. Dan McCarthy, Dublin, stated that the counties which had representatives on the team should play-off to decide ownership of the Shield. Having provided fifteen of the seventeen players for the Leinster team the Kilkenny Board officers would not accept this decision and appealed the matter to Central Council. A prolonged hotly contested debate took place before the Chairman, Alderman Nowlan, ruled that the Leinster Council had erred in its decision and should revisit the issue.

At a special meeting held on April 25th the Leinster Council decided by 8 votes to 6 to hand over the Shield to Kilkenny. Kilkenny Co. Board of the GAA decided that the Shield should be presented to the Corporation to be put on display in the Council Chamber. It is worth recording that a member of the winning Railway Shield team was Bob O'Keeffe. Bob, originally from Mooncoin but then living in Co. Laois, was a member of the Laois team and was picked by the Kilkenny selectors to represent Leinster. He was on the Laois team in 1915 when they won their only Senior Hurling Championship. He later had a very successful career in GAA administration being Treasurer and later President of the Leinster Council before his election as National President of the Association in 1935. The **'Inter-provincial Hurling Challenge Shield'** was subsequently presented to Kilkenny Corporation at a meeting of that body on February 6th 1911 by the Secretary of Kilkenny County GAA Board, Mr. Dan O'Connell. Mr. O'Connell and Mr. John Lalor represented the Board. Addressing a very crowded Council Chamber including the Mayor, Alderman Thomas Cantwell, J. P. and Alderman Nowlan, Mr. O'Connell gave details the series of matches that were played over the previous four years and expressed the satisfaction of the

Co.Board members at the achievements of the hurlers and the support received from the general public. In presenting the Shield to the Mayor Mr. O'Connell stated **'apart from the fitness of the place it is but just to this corporate body that they should be made the guardians of the trophies won by the Gaels of Kilkenny'.**

In accepting the Shield the Mayor thanked the Board for their thoughtfulness in presenting the wonderful trophy to the Corporation and assured them it would be displayed with pride in the Council Chamber. He also stated that **'the Shield was further enhanced by having the name of our illustrious Alderman Nowlan'** engraved on it. The Mayor then paid tribute to the achievements of Alderman Nowlan both at local and national level and thanked him on behalf of the Corporation for his untiring efforts on behalf of the people of Kilkenny and of the youth of Ireland. When the deputation had withdrawn the Corporation's Engineer, Mr. Murphy, submitted a design for an oak casing and frame for the Shield which he had obtained from Mr. Patrick Corcoran[19], Patrick St. Mr. Murphy stated that the cost would be £12. The members considered the casing to be very suitable and very reasonably priced and agreed to accept the offer from Mr. Corcoran. The Shield adorned the Council Chamber for many years and more recently has been in the safe custody of the Lory Meagher Centre in Tullaroan.

The Railway Shield

Central Council again found itself in a conflict situation in 1912. The matter concerned the playing of the 1911 All-Ireland hurling final between Kilkenny and Limerick. The match was fixed for the Athletic Grounds in Cork on February 18th. On the day the pitch was flooded due to very heavy overnight rain and the referee declared it unplayable. A sub-committee of the GAA re-fixed the match for April 21st in Thurles. Limerick objected to the choice of venue and appealed the decision to the Annual Congress due to be held in Dublin on Easter Sunday, April 7th. After a long, intense and fiery debate Congress upheld the decision of Central Council but Limerick adamantly refused to play at any venue except Cork.

Limerick was suspended and the Munster Council was asked to nominate a team to play Kilkenny so as to recover some of the expenditure lost due to the non- playing of the final. Tipperary was asked to play since they had been beaten by Limerick. The match was played at Dungarvan and was won by Kilkenny, 3-3 to 2-1, who were then declared All-Ireland champions for 1911. As a result of the conflicting views on the above dispute and the strong feelings raised it is not too surprising that all the main officerships were contested – an unusual occurrence.

Alderman Nowlan was opposed by J. J. Walsh, Cork, but won comfortably on a vote, 53 to 19. Luke O'Toole was re-elected as Secretary as were Dan Fraher, Waterford and Michael Crowe, Dublin, as trustees.

A big effort was now made to get the 1912 championships under-way so as to avoid once again an overspill into the following year. Kilkenny beat both Wexford and Laois to qualify for the All-Ireland final. Cork won through in Munster having beaten Tipperary in the final, 5-1 to 3-1, after a great contest. The final was fixed to November 17th at Jones' Road. An attendance of 20,000 was present and the gate receipts were £589, a new record for the Association. In what was regarded as the best and most exciting final played to date Kilkenny came from behind in the closing stages to win by one point. This was the last final to be played involving seventeen players on each side – henceforth it would be fifteen a-side and so it has remained.

1913, as we have seen, was the year when the Jones' Road lands were acquired by the Association. At Congress on Sunday, March 23rd at Dublin City Hall some important rule changes were passed which have withstood the test of time, e. g.:

'That a distinctive county colour be compulsory for inter-county, inter-provincial and All-Ireland contests, such colours to be approved by the provincial Council concerned and registered with Central Council'

'That the number of players per team be reduced from 17 to 15; this rule to come into effect on May 1st'.

Also passed was a motion to invest £700 in Railway Stock so as to place the Association 'in a position of procuring further railway facilities and of obtaining other financial concessions'. This was a political/commercial investment. The availability of train services was of crucial importance in popularising the games by ensuring large attendances at the big matches. The rail companies put on 'special trains' for the important matches and we read that sometimes in excess of 3,000 patrons were on board. The Association members felt that by investing in the company they had more leverage in getting trains for matches and in doing deals in regard to the cost of the fare. We have referred to attendances of 15 -20,000 at finals in Jones' Road in those now distant days. Certainly the availability of rail travel made that possible.

The following aspiratory motion from the Cork Board was also passed:

'That in order to induce our members to use our national language, we appoint a Committee to devise a plan whereby an additional portion of the business of the Association will year by year be done in Ár dTeanga Féin'

Attendant to the above the rule book was translated into Irish and **'a collection of suitable terms in Irish for use by players was included'**

CHAPTER 25

There have been many milestone events in the development of the GAA since its birth in 1884. Arguably the decision in 1913 to purchase the property which was to become Croke Park was one of the greatest. A meeting on January 5th 1913 made a game changing decision regarding the Croke Memorial Fund. It was decided to organise an inter-county tournament in both hurling and football to be played in the early months of the year and that the entire gate receipts would go to the memorial fund. The tournaments were a great success from both a sporting and financial point of view. Louth and Kerry contested the football final on March 4th and the match ended in a draw. The replay took place on June 29th and attracted 32,000 spectators to the Jones' Road grounds who paid £1192 to see Kerry win comfortably. Kilkenny and Tipperary played the hurling final in Dungarvan in which Tipperary were victorious.

The quarterly meeting on July 6th was informed by the President, Alderman Nowlan, that the tournaments had been a financial success beyond their expectations and that the total receipts amounted to £2,735-3-4 and the expenses were £862-17-1, leaving a credit balance of £1872-6-3. This added to the balance already in the fund, £493-5-4, made a total of £2,365-11-7. The original target envisioned for the fund was £1,000. Central Council now had an unexpected problem as the members had to decide how best to use the monies available.

A special meeting was held on July 27th and it was decided to al-lot £1,000 for a statue of Dr. Croke to be erected in Liberty Square in Thurles and on the proposal of Alderman Nowlan it was agreed **'that £300 be advanced towards the refurbishment of the Confraternity Hall in Thurles, which had been damaged by fire, on condition that it be called Croke Memorial Hall'**. The minutes further record a proposal **'that the remainder of the funds be devoted to the purchase of grounds in Dublin to be called Croke Memorial Park Grounds'** was carried by 6 votes to 3. Secretary O Toole was directed to make enquiries regarding available properties and to report to the next meeting.

The Council met again on August 17th. The secretary reported that the sub-committee members **'had visited several grounds around Dublin'** but only two could considered as suitable – Jones' Road and Elm Park, Merrion. Details were presented to the meeting in relation to the extent, general suitability and asking price of each. It was decided that all members of the Council should inspect Elm Park; Jones' Road was well known to all as the association had been playing many games there over recent years. It was noted that the Jones' Road property had added value in that two houses existed on the site. The matter was debated at two further meetings and was further progressed at a meeting on October 4th when Mr. Crowe proposed that Council make an offer of £3, 500 to Mr. Frank Dineen, the owner, for the Jones' Road grounds. This was seconded by Mr. Lawler. The offer was to pay Mr. Dineen £1,500 in cash and accept liability for the mortgage of £2,000 which Dineen had negotiated with the Munster and Leinster bank. The meeting appointed a deputation to finalise the deal with Frank Dineen 'and to make application to the bank for a loan of £2,000 to enable the Council to purchase Jones' Road Sports Ground.

The Council meeting on December 1st took the following decisions:

Luke O Toole was appointed manager of Croke Park at an annual salary of £75,
Patrick Martin was selected as caretaker and was allotted one of the houses on the property.

At the meeting on January 4th it was further decided that:

The second house be given to Luke O Toole 'at a nominal rent',
an office be fitted out in one of the rooms attached in the pavilion where council meetings can be held in future,
the tenancy of 68 Upper O'Connell St. be surrendered,
a grounds and Finance Committee was appointed in connection with Croke Park.

By a deed signed on October 13th the title of the property was conveyed to the trustees for the Association. The trustees were: Alderman James Nowlan, Luke J. O Toole, Michael F. Crowe, Dublin, Dan Fraher, Dungarvan, John Collins, Dublin, Tom Kenny, Craughwell, Co. Galway, John J. Horgan, Dublin, and John E. Malone, Ennis, Co. Clare.

Unexpected difficulties for Central Council immediately arose. The Tipperary Board threatened to legally challenge the Council's decision regarding the use of the Fund. They stated that it was their understanding that all the monies raised were intended for the Thurles memorial and demanded that the Fund would not be used as planned by the Council until it was discussed at Congress at Easter 1914. This was indeed drastic action by the Board; there was not unanimous agreement in the county at this course of action – the South Board had voted by a clear majority its disapproval of the procedure. After much negotiation and diplomacy on the part of the officers of Central Council a compromise was reached whereby the Council agreed to increase the allocation towards the Thurles project. Local difficulties later arose regarding the site and the size of the monument and delayed its implementation.

Many years later, on St. Patrick's Day, 1920, the foundation stone for the Croke Memorial was laid by Most Rev. Dr. Harty, Archbishop of Cashel. Alderman Jim Nowlan, Pesident of the GAA presided and there were representatives from all parts of the country.

Some readers may be interested in the earlier history of the property. I now include an extract from **'Bláth'**, the pamphlet produced for the **'Official Opening of the New Hogan Stand in the 75th Year of the Gaelic Athletic Association Sunday, June 7th, 1959'**

By a deed dated 10th December, 1829, the venerable John Torrens and Rev. Henry Brownrigg leased to John Bradley **'an orchard, dwelling house, yard and garden together with the fields adjoining'** containing twelve acres and twenty four perches, statute measure. The land was described as being **'on the east side of the Royal canal and on the north side of Bally-bough Lane in the barony of Coolock, Parish of St. George and**

county of Dublin'. The lease was for five hundred years from
29th September 1829, and the rent seventy-five pounds a year.
By another deed of 16th of April, 1864, Robert Fowler leased
to Maurice Butterly a plot containing 21 acres one rood and 12
perches statute measure for five hundred years from 1st May,
1863, at a rent of £175 a year. This land was described as being
**'on the south side of Clonliffe Road in the parish of St. George
and county of Dublin'.** The two plots of ground comprised in these
two leases were adjoining. In the course of time they were acquired
by one owner. The two deeds referred to are the Association's roots
of title to Croke Park.

From time to time the area comprised in the two leases was
reduced by lettings for building and by compulsory acquisition
of the portion by the railway wall and at the canal end by the
then Midland Great Western Railway Company and the Great
Southern and Western Railway Company. The rents at the time
were reduced or adjusted. The history of these transactions is
long and involved. Coming down to more recent times we find
that in 1894 a company called the City and Suburban Racecourse
and Amusements Grounds Limited was incorporated. That
company purchased the property in the same year. For some
years it let the grounds for sports meetings and whippet racing,
a sport that had a brief popularity in Dublin. But the company
proved to be a financial failure and in 1900 it decided to wind
up. Meanwhile the Company had on various occasions let the
grounds to the GAA.

The first All-Ireland Finals were played there in 1896,
while the Finals for 1895, both in Hurling and Football,
were played on the same day. The property was put up
for auction in 1906. It was described in the auctioneer's
advertisement as then consisting in all of 14 acres and 17.5
perches, the total annual rents payable being then £93-17s
-10d. By a deed of 17th December, 1908, the property was
conveyed to Frank Brazil Dineen, described as of Albert
Villas, in the city of Dublin, for £3,250. What he purchased
was the Croke Park grounds as it now is (remember this
was written in 1959) and also the Belvedere grounds adjoining

the boundary wall on the Cusack Stand side. At the time it was all one ground with no boundary wall between.

Frank B. Dineen was a Kerryman from Ballylanders, he was a journalist employed by the **'Freeman's Journal'**. He was a noted athlete and had been throughout his life active in the G.A.A., having at different times held the offices of Vice-President, President and Secretary of the Association. He was President 1895-98 when he resigned to become Secretary, 1898-1901, and was the only person to hold both offices in the Association. He died suddenly at his office desk on Good Friday, April 21st 1916 aged 54 years.

Mr. Dineen's purpose was not to make profit out of the purchase but to hold it for the GAA. At that time the G.A.A.'s finances did not permit it to consider acquiring the property. Meanwhile Mr. Dineen had to borrow money to purchase and hold it. In 1910 he was compelled, in order to reduce the debt due to the Bank by way of mortgage on the premises, to sell four acres and two roods to the Jesuit Fathers for the sum of £1,090.

The role of Frank Dineen in the story of Croke Park has surely not got the recognition it deserves. It was fitting that at the conclusion of the development of the northern end of the stadium in 1995 part of the old Hill 16 terrace was renamed the Dineen terrace. It is also of interest to record that in advance of the development of the Cusack Stand side of the grounds in 1991, the Croke Park management bought back the Belvedere Sports Ground eighty one years after it had been sold by Frank Dineen.

Many years later it was stated **'that the GAA had a competitor for the venue; the Catholic Archbishop of Dublin had been reputedly negotiating with Dineen to purchase the grounds for the site of a proposed metropolitan cathedral.'** (Nolan, p.101)

Nationalist sentiment had been increasing throughout the country from 1898 after a year of high profile commemoration events on the anniversary of 1798[20]. The Royal visits at the beginning of the century further induced feelings of resentment and impatience by nationally minded people at the lack of progress on Home Rule.

Meanwhile Arthur Griffith was developing a political philosophy less militaristic than that of the IRB and less indulgent than that of the IPP. Griffith was a journalist who produced and edited his own newspaper, the **'United Irishman'** and therein he defined his ideas and made them available to his readership.

At a meeting held in the Rotunda in Dublin on November 28th 1905 with Griffith presiding the Sinn Fein party was formed. **'On that occasion the Dublin GAA clubs marched in military formation and provided stewards to marshal the 8,000 in attendance'** (Nolan, p. 101). While branches came into being subsequently in various towns throughout the country, its development was erratic, it did not inspire the masses (Garvin).

In 1907 James Nowlan chaired a meeting in Kilkenny at which a motion was passed favouring the Irish-Ireland principles of Sinn Fein. This event once again raised questions about the non-political policy of the GAA. Nowlan however clarified that he was present as an Alderman of Kilkenny Corporation and not in his capacity as President of the GAA.

The Home Rule Bill of 1912 prompted the formation of the Ulster Volunteers in January 1913 as a military force to resist the introduction of the Bill. Later that year, on November 25th a huge meeting of Nationalists, including many high profile GAA members, was held at The Rotunda in Dublin when the Irish Volunteers was formed. Amongst the speakers at that meeting was Luke O' Toole, General Secretary of the GAA, and also present was Harry Boland, then chairman if the Dublin GAA Board. Moore, p. 47, states **"the GAA President, James Nowlan, a member of the IRB, is reported as advising GAA members to join the Volunteers and 'learn to shoot straight"**. Some commentators have suggested the GAA and the Volunteers were indistinguishable such was the overlap of membership. However the Association's leadership consistently emphasised that members were free to join any organisation but did not represent or speak for the Association. In December 1913 an informal approach was made to the Association seeking public support for the

Volunteer movement. The approach was rejected. (O'Toole,p 85)

At the outbreak of World War 1, John Redmond gave a commitment to support the Allied cause and recommended that members of the Volunteers should join the British Army. Many thousands did so to the strong disapproval of the IRB and Sinn Fein wings of the movement and resulted in the movement being split. Many clubs were decimated by the loss of players, some joined the British Army and some were unavailable at weekends due to training commitments with the Volunteers. The tensions this created in clubs and counties led to the fear of a split amongst the Associations membership. That this did not happen is indicative of the extreme loyalty of the members to one another and to the GAA.

1913 was also the year when bitter disputes between employers and workers, about working conditions and wages, came to a head in Dublin City. This culminated in the Great Lockout of workers which continued for several months. Great distress and poverty resulted for thousands of workers and their families. The Dublin GAA Board organised matches to raise much needed funds for the strikers many of whom were their members.

A lesser and shorter episode of a similar nature took place in Wexford town in 1911. The local Board of the GAA organised benefit matches and the Leinster Council of the GAA also supported a fundraising effort. (Enright, p. 31)

On the playing fields 1913 turned out to be a wonderful year for the Kilkenny Hurlers. For the second time the team was attempting to win three All-Irelands in a row. The campaign was quite long and included two trips across the Irish Sea to play teams from Britain, one in Glasgow and one in Liverpool. One hundred years ago such journeys must have been demanding and exciting. The team finally qualified for the Final against the **'Toomavara Greyhounds'** representing Tipperary. The match was fixed for Jones' Road on November 2nd. Ryall gives a full account of the match which Kilkenny won – the scores being 2-4 to 1-2. Great excitement prevailed amongst the Kilkenny players and supporters who stormed the pitch.

On the day, back home in Kilkenny, crowds of people gathered in High St. to get news of the match. The **'Kilkenny People'** described it thus:

At about 4.45 pm a telegram was received through the courtesy of the 'Kilkenny People'. As the specified time arrived for the arrival of the wire intense excitement took hold. When the news finally broke there

was loud and prolonged cheering and steps were immediately begun to arrange a fitting reception for the returning champions.

The following evening the Corporation met for their monthly meeting. A motion of congratulations to the team was proposed by Mr. Magennis and he went on to suggest that the freedom of the City should be conferred on the fifteen players. The Borough Treasurer interrupted to remind the members that when someone is given the Freedom of the City £3 stamp duty must be paid to the Government and if the fifteen players were given the honour the cost would be £45 - a huge sum one hundred years ago. Strong views were expressed in regard to giving money to the Government and it was also questioned if it was good use of money and that perhaps it should be given to the players instead. One member questioned if the team was treated as a unit would one payment of £3 suffice. Eventually a motion was carried agreeing to give the Freedom of the City to the team; the options were to honour the team by conferring the honour on the team captain or to honour the team as a unit. The question of the tax to be investigated.

Frank Dineen, 1862 - 1916

CHAPTER 27

The 1914 Congress was held at Dublin City Hall on Easter Sunday, April 9th. As referred to earlier the dispute relating to the Croke Memorial was dealt with satisfactorily.

The following motion was passed re All-Ireland finals:

'That future All-Ireland Championship finals be played at Croke Memorial Park on fixed Sundays in each year, one on the first Sunday in September and the other on the fourth Sunday'.

This decision was complied with up to recent times.

At the March meeting of the Kilkenny Co. GAA Board the Secretary, Mr. John Lalor stated he had received a letter from Mr. W. Hanrahan, Sec. of the Leinster Council which read;

A Chara, the following resolution was passed at the recent Leinster Convention of the GAA – 'That it is an instruction from this Convention to the County Committees to interview the heads of colleges in their counties and press forward the rights of Irish games by all means in their power'. You are to bring this to your Committee for the purpose of having the necessary steps taken at the earliest opportunity.

The following exchange then too place;

Chairman, Mr. John Dunphy – there is only one college here, St. Kierans, and I believe Irish games are being played there. Alderman Nowlan – Yes but they do not enter for the Leinster College's competition. I think a resolution should be passed asking them to enter for that competition.

On the suggestion of the Chairman it was agreed to write to the President of the College bringing to his notice the fact that no team from the College took part in the Leinster Colleges

Championship. How things changed; the other colleges must have wished they stayed out!!!

In Kilkenny a unique event took place in the City Hall on the night of March 16th. A public presentation was made to the all-conquering county hurling team that had just completed a three-in-a-row series of All-Ireland victories and had won seven All-Irelands over the previous ten years.

Earlier, public subscriptions had been invited to enable a presentation to be made and generous sums of money were received from Kilkenny people both at home and abroad.

On the occasion a huge number of people were present as the Mayor, Alderman John Maginnes, welcomed the players, members of the County Board, his colleagues on the Corporation and the general public. The Mayor and some members of the Corporation made congratulatory speeches after which each of twenty players was made a presentation of a cheque for £14 and eight gold medals won in recent competitions. The evening concluded with the singing of **'A Nation Once Again'**.

The political landscape greatly influenced the life of the GAA in 1914/15. The Volunteer movement continued to prosper with vast numbers of young men now joining. A branch of the Irish Volunteers was formed in Kilkenny on March 6th. It is interesting to read the following interpretation sent to Dublin Castle by the County Inspector of the RIC:

'The Irish Volunteer movement which was inaugurated in Kilkenny City on March 6th last by Sir Roger Casement and Mr. McDonagh has made steady progress and is mainly supported by members drawn from the artisan and labouring classes, shop assistants, clerks etc.. The merchants and more respectable classes have held aloof from the movement so far as they are unwilling to be brought into contact for drill purposes with persons whom they consider inferior to them socially. The movement has however the sympathy and approval of all classes of Nationalists in and around the City including the R. C. clergy. The total strength of the city branch is 240 members and the average number that attend the drills is 150. The drill takes place thrice weekly with an occasional

route march. So far arms are not carried. There is only one drill master, ex Sagt. Thos. Connolly of the Kilkenny militia – Peter Deloughrey and Alderman James Nolan are the only persons of local influence who take an active part in organising the corps. A battalion is being organised in Callan and up to the present 200 have applied to be enrolled.

The Redmondites organised a massive parade for Easter Sunday 1915 in which it was estimated that 25,000 of the National Volunteers took part. The GAA Congress, as usual fixed for that date, commenced earlier than usual so as to finish at lunchtime and thereby permit the delegates to participate in the parade. By their actions you know them!!

A further opportunity for the Nationalists to show strength was presented on the death of Jermiagh O'Donovan Rossa, the veteran Fenian. Rossa had died in America and was brought home for burial. The body was taken to City Hall for a lying-in-state and afterwards to Glasnevin cemetery for burial on August 1st. Thousands of Volunteers, from all parts of the country, paraded in tribute and after the burial listened to Patrick Pearse deliver the panegyric. That speech which had taken a lot of time in preparation, was, and is still considered to be, his masterpiece. He recalled the deeds of the Fenian forefathers and linked them to his own time thus further inspiring in his listeners the republican spirit.

Not surprisingly the RIC were compiling their reports from around the country and had concluded that the GAA was very supportive of the separatist movement, i.e. the Irish Volunteers. Kilkenny was listed as one of a few counties where this was particularly the case.

Central Council and the Provincial Councils were continuing with their programmes of championship and tournament matches. In a few counties, as already stated, club activity was hampered but overall GAA life went on more or less as usual. Leix surprised Kilkenny by beating them, 4-1 to 2-6, in the Leinster senior hurling semi-final played at Tullamore. The Munster final was a torrid affair between Cork and Limerick. Neither team scored in the first half and when a fracas developed in the second half the referee, Tim Ryan, Chairman of the Tipperary Board, called off the match. Cork was leading 2-1 to 0-0. At a subsequent meeting of Central Council Cork were awarded the match on a 5 to 4 vote.

At the May meeting of the Kilkenny Co. Board the appointment of selection committees was one of the items on the agenda. The following members were appointed as selectors for the Senior Hurling team;

Alderman James Nowlan, S. Walton, Tullaroan, P.Lanigan, Erin's Own, R. Walsh or J. Delahunty, Mooncoin, J. Rochford, John Lalor and the Chairman (Mr. D. J. Gorey).

Michael Collins speaking to some of the Kilkenny players and officials before the start of the 1921 Leinster Final against Dublin.
From left; Paddy Donoghue(Dicksboro), Mattie Power(Dicksboro), Dick Grace(Tullaroan), Michael Joyce(Callan), Martin Egan(Threecastles), Bill Kenny(Lisdowney), Jack Holohan(from Johnstown, played with Tullaroan),Michael Collins and Harry Boland.

CHAPTER 28

1916 commenced as usual with a flurry of GAA activity. On January 31st the Leix hurlers were entertained at a banquet at Maryborough to celebrate their 1915 All-Ireland hurling victory. The Kilkenny county final of 1915 took place at James' Park where Tullaroan beat Dicksbouragh, 7-2 to 2-2. In the Kilkenny senior football final of 1915 took place again at James' Park on April 2nd between Glenmore and Coolagh. It ended in a draw, 1-1 each side. The replay was again a draw, 1-0 each side. The second replay played at Waterford was again a draw, Glenmore 1-3, Coolagh 2-0. Finally a result was delivered at James' Park on October 16 when Glenmore won, 1-0 to 0-2. This was the start of a remarkable winning sequence by a great Glenmore team that proved almost unbeatable over the following 10 years.

In the early part of 1916 the British Government introduced an Entertainment Tax on sporting events. Some exemptions were allowed for and in an effort to qualify for exemption the GAA sent a deputation to London to meet the Chancellor. The deputation consisted of President Nowlan, Secretary O'Toole and Frank Dineen. They were introduced to the Chancellor by John Redmond, M.P. Leader of the IPP and Mr. John O'Connor M.P. The delegation failed to convince the officials of the justification for exemption which they clearly had on at least two grounds laid down in the Act namely; that the games were promoted and organised to revive national pastimes, and also that the Association was a non-profit body.

The Kilkenny county convention elected Sean Gibbons, Clomanto, as chairman, he replaced Denis J Gorey of Burnchurch. Gibbons had a long innings as chairman, 1916 – 1922, and again 1929 – 1941. The election of Sean Gibbons did not escape the attention of the Constabulary. In his monthly report to Dublin Castle on November 1st 1916 County Inspector, P. C. Power stated:

The Political organisations remain unchanged except that John Gibbons, an admired Sinn Feiner and released interned prisoner has been elected President of the County Committee

GAA instead of Denis J Gorey, J. P. Gibbons had not previously taken an active part in GAA matters and it is believed his election was a consequence of his advanced views which shows sympathy between the GAA and Sinn Fein propaganda.

Congress was scheduled for Easter Sunday, April 23rd. Alderman Nowlan went to Dublin on the Saturday because of the death the previous day of Frank Dineen. The meeting was well attended, there being upwards of seventy delegates present. No major decisions were taken. The Entertainment Tax issue was discussed and the report of the delegation to London was considered. The Council decided to convene a special Congress later if the matter was not successfully resolved. James Nowlan did not return to Kilkenny that evening. We have a most comprehensive record of his activities over the following week from the Witness Statement of Willie Walsh[21]. Witness statements were taken by the Bureau of Military History and are stored in the Military Archive, Cathal Brugha St., Dublin[22]. I now quote some relevant parts of Walsh's statement;

I was born in Waterford on 19th December 1879. I came of Fenian stock, my grandfather being an old Fenian.
My first connection with the national movement was through the Gaelic Athletic Association and the Gaelic League which I joined about the year 1900.
About the year 1909 I was at a hurling match in Maryboro (now Portlaoise) when I met M F Crowe of Limerick, a prominent GAA official at the time. He was an organiser for the Irish Republican Brotherhood and he had a chat with me about joining. I agreed to join so he swore me in there and then, gave me a copy of the oath and told me to start enrolling new members down the Waterford way.
I was appointed 'Head Centre'[23] by Crowe for Waterford.
I administered the oath to thirty one men all of whom were connected with the GAA or the Gaelic League in Waterford. The oath was usually administered by me at GAA matches where I used to meet these men.
In Waterford City I started the John Mitchell Hurling Club which really was intended as a cloak for IRB activities in that city.

In common with all the other members of the IRB in Waterford I joined the National Volunteers on their establishment in Waterford in 1914. A man named Bob Kelly (known as 'Colonel' Kelly) was officer-in-charge at that time.

Early in Easter week 1916 there were rumours that the Rising was to come off on Good Friday.

Confusing messages were coming through however, so having discussed the matter with some of my colleagues, Peadar Woods, J D Walsh, Sean Matthews and P. Brazil, it was decided that I would go to Dublin on the Saturday. I was a county delegate to the annual GAA Congress which was being held in Croke House, Jones' Road on Easter Sunday so I was going to Dublin at the weekend anyway. I should explain here that I had arranged to wire Peadar Woods in Waterford 'going to Fairyhouse races' if I learned that the Rising was off, and if the Rising was on I was to wire him "going to Waterford". On Easter Sunday I met Harry Boland at the GAA Convention and asked him if he had any definitive news about the Rising. He told me he wasn't sure what was going to happen. He could not give me any definite information. We waited until 2am on Easter Monday in Croke House, the residence of Luke O'Toole, at that time the secretary of the GAA, for any further information but none came. On Easter Monday I thought that all operations were off so I wired Peadar at Waterford about 10.30am saying "Going to Fairyhouse today".

I met J.J. Nowlan who was President of the GAA then and a Kilkennyman, and went for a walk. We decided to go home on the afternoon train. When we came back to town (Dublin) after our walk at about 1.30pm we heard that the Rising had started and when we came to Usher's Quay we heard shooting down around the Four Courts.

We had dinner in a house on the quays in the neighbourhood of Usher's Quay and then we went to Kingsbridge railway station with a view to getting home as we didn't know what might be happening there. At Kingsbridge there was a big crowd of passengers. After waiting a long time we were all informed that there would be no trains going out that day so we went off to the house of a friend and slept there that night.

The following morning we made our way across to Phibsboro on the north-west side of the city, and went to the house of Harry Kenny in Connaught St., Phibsboro. Harry was a Kilkenny man and a great GAA man. He put us up for Tuesday night and for the rest of the week until the Rising finished I stayed with J.J. Nowlan in the house of people by the name of Liddy, near Harry Kenny's house and friends of his.

During Easter week I made several attempts to get to the city but was stopped by cordons of British military who would not allow me to pass through.

I returned to Waterford by train on Monday, May 1st and immediately on my arrival in Waterford I was arrested at the railway station by a detective named Organ and handed over to the British military. I was then brought to the military barracks in Ballybricken, Waterford, questioned, searched and kept in Ballybricken for about three weeks when I was released unconditionally.

British Occupation Forces, Dublin, 1916

CHAPTER 29

On May 3rd a large contingent of military and police arrived in Kilkenny, cordoned off the streets and a general arrest of **'suspects'** commenced. Alderman Nowlan did not return to Kilkenny until May 4th. He was arrested as he crossed John's Bridge on his way to his home at about 6.15pm, having come off the Dublin train. He was taken to John St. Barracks before being transferred to Kilkenny jail under escort by six soldiers with rifles and fixed bayonets. Many more were arrested in the City and environs on the following days including Michael Ryan, James Nowlan's cousin. Meanwhile a large number of British Cavalry and Infantry had arrived in the City to reinforce the British Army in the Kilkenny Barracks. On May 9th all those arrested over the previous days were marched, under heavy escort of British Infantry, Cavalry and RIC, from the jail to the railway station and put on a special train for Dublin. They were then marched from Kingsbridge Station to Richmond Barracks and put into barrack rooms. Conditions were very crowded and uncomfortable there.

On the 12th the following Kilkenny prisoners were removed from Richmond Barracks and brought to Wakefield Prison in West Yorkshire:

Denis Barry, Monster House,
Patrick Burke (Snr), Wolfe Tone St.,
Edward Comerford, Wellington Quay,
Joseph Coyne, Bishop's Hill,
Laurence De Loughrey, Parliament St.,
William Denn, Talbot's Inch,
Tom Furlong, Michael St.,
Sean Gibbons, Freshford,
John Harte, Blanchfield's Park,
Maurice Higgins, Upper John St.,
Martin Kealy, Blanchfield's Park,
James Lalor, Friary St.,
James Madigan, Abbey St.,
Thomas Neary, Poulgower,

Alderman Jim Nowlan, Bishop's Hill,
Michael O'Dwyer, John St.,
Patrick Parsons, Wolfe Tone St.,
Michael Purcell, High St.,
Michael Ryan, Bishop's Hill,
Charlie Smith, Maudlin St.,
William Stephens, c/o Burkes High St.,
Laurence Walsh, Dunmore[24]

Together with other high profile GAA people, Michael Collins, Harry Boland, Austin Stack and hundreds of ordinary members, they were given prison sentences. Something in the region of two thousand persons were sent to British jails. Surprisingly Luke O'Toole was not arrested though he must have been on various lists of **'suspects'** on RIC files. Hundreds were sent to Frongoch Prison in Wales. Here the prisoners, including Dick Fitzgerald the legendary Kerry footballer, arranged football matches amongst themselves.

Amongst the leaders of the 1916 Rising arrested and executed it is not surprising that some were high profile GAA men including Patrick Pearse, Con Colbert, Sean McDermott, Eamonn Ceannt and Michael O'Hanrahan. Some other prominent GAA people arrested and sentenced to death were J. J. Walsh, Cork, Wexford man Sean Etchingham from Enniscorthy, Con O'Donovan and Jack Shouldice both from Dublin; they however had their sentences commuted to terms of penal servitude.

In response to a question in the House of Commons on Monday, May 29th, Mr. Tennant stated that Alderman Nowlan, Kilkenny, **'was at present detained at Wakefield and that all cases were being investigated as rapidly as possible'.**

Most of the prisoners were released, in small groups, in the month of June. Nowlan got his freedom in June 19th having been selected for particularly severe treatment including lengthy periods of solitary confinement.

A meeting of Central Council was held on May 28th. J. J. Hogan, President of the Leinster Council, presided in the absence of President Nowlan. The minutes do not have any reference to the reason for his absence!! The main item on the agenda was to formulate a statement in response to an allegation made by the Secretary of State, Sir Matthew Nathan, that the Association had been involved in the planning of the Rising. The Association's response, issued to the press and to the Rebellion Commission repudiated **'press reports before the Rebellion Commission by those giving evidence endeavouring to connect the GAA with the Irish Volunteers and the Citizen Army'.** The Council also quoted the Association's rule that they **'shall be strictly non-political and non-sectarian Association. No political questions of any kind shall be raised at any of its meetings and neither Central Council, Provincial Councils, County Committees nor clubs shall take part in any political movement'.**

The statement concludes **'Central Council strongly protests against the misrepresentations of the aims and objects of the Gaelic Athletic Association as tendered to the Commission by Sir Matthew Nathan and other witnesses, and thinks that all such allegations should, at least, be accompanied by definite proofs'.**

The meeting also discussed the Entertainment Tax issue and instructed the secretary to write to John O'Connor, M.P. asking him to raise the matter again with the British Government. A meeting of November 26th was informed of a report from Mr. John O'Connor in which he stated that it was intimated by the Revenue Commissioners that the Association would be exempt provided that some rules in the official guide were deleted and others altered. Such a move was unanimously rejected.

This matter dragged on for a further year. A special Congress was called for August 6th 1917 and a unanimous decision was reached, that **'no amusement tax whatever be paid no matter against whom proceedings might be taken'** with some delegates suggesting that **'members of the Association with means should stand aside from the Association for the present so as to give no opportunity where by the tax might be recouped'.** The Association did not pay the tax for the remaining years of British control and the Central Council minutes do not seem to refer to the matter again during that period. A tax issue did surface again under our native government in the mid-1920s. The matter was, from the GAA perspective, satisfactorily resolved after some serious political campaigning.

CHAPTER 30

Understandably, due to political involvement by so many members, the games schedule was badly disrupted during Spring and early Summer of 1916. However by July fairly normal games activity had resumed. Kilkenny and Tipperary qualified for the All-Ireland final in hurling while Wexford again won through to the final to meet Mayo who were contesting their first final. It should be stated that Kerry withdrew from the championships that year due to the absence of so many players and administrators who were in prisons for political reasons. The finals were both fixed for December, the hurling to be on 3rd and the football on the 16th, both at Croke Park.

The hurling was however deferred to January 21st 1917. The reason for this was the decision of the Railway Companies not to run 'special' trains to GAA matches – this appears to be in retaliation by the Government over the Association's stance on the tax issue. The Association strongly resisted this ruling and sent a deputation to London lead by Nowlan to meet the Chief Secretary, Mr. H.E. Dukes, but it was all to no avail. Trains did run to Dublin but normal fares were charged. In the event both finals drew very small crowds – 5,000 for the hurling final compared to 14,000 the previous year, and 3,000 for the football final as against 27,000 in 1915. It should be said that the 1915 football between Wexford and Kerry was the glamour match of the decade. The attendances obviously resulted in the Association taking a big financial hit on the finals. Tipperary won the hurling final after a tremendous match, 5-4 to 3-2. Wexford won their second football final in a row, Wexford 2-4, Mayo 1-2.

Political activities and nationalist feelings strongly dominated the lives of many in 1917. This was reflected in the success of a number of Sinn Fein candidates, including W. T. Cosgrave in Kilkenny, who won seats at the expense of the IPP. On April 8th Congress was held in camera for the first time – no Press or public were admitted. The Junior Championships were suspended for the year. No other decisions of major importance were made. A limited report of proceedings was later released to the Press.

On the playing fields the championships, both national and local, were curtailed to a greater or lesser extent. The Kilkenny hurling and football championships did not take place in 1917 or 1918. Wexford again won the All-Ireland football championship when they beat Clare, 0-9 to 0-5.

In hurling Tipperary and Dublin got to the final. Tipperary were strong favourites but were 'turned over' by a young Dublin team, 5-4 to 4-2. On the Dublin team was a young Kilkenny man, Tommy Moore[25], who was to become a central figure in Dublin GAA life in later years.

1918 was a year of intense political activity for the Association. Games were played and meetings held in the first half of the year but for many clubs/counties political involvement became the main focus as the year wore on. The Annual Congress was held on March 31st in the Mansion House, Dublin. As in the previous year Press and public were not admitted. At the start of the meeting Harry Boland 'asked for information regarding alleged deputations that waited on the Commander-in-Chief of the military forces in London'. (Minutes, p. 425). De Burca (p.110) writes **'a long and acrimonious discussion ended with the passing, by twenty seven votes to twenty five, of a vote of censure on Central Council for such contacts; however a substantial number of delegates, possibly as many as thirty, abstained'**. The criticism was particularly directed at Nowlan and O'Toole. Harry Boland, James Nowlan and Luke O'Toole were close friends and were on the same wavelength in regard to their separatist political beliefs. This conscientious verbal feud, related to the approach adopted to resolve a political confrontation with the Government, was a foretaste of the calamitous divisions which took place a few years later amongst our people during the civil war period.

When it came to the subsequent election of officers all were returned unopposed suggesting that the main body of the representatives accepted the approach adopted by the leadership. There is no record of any decisions of note taken at the meeting.

CHAPTER 31

The next confrontation with the authorities was not far away. In April the Government introduced a Bill which became law extending conscription to Ireland. There was instant reaction throughout the country. All political leaders, the Church, the Unions and the GAA let it be known that there would be massive resistance if this new law was enforced. A meeting of Central Council of the GAA was called and adopted a resolution which stated **'that we pledge ourselves to resist by any and every means in our power the attempted conscription of Irish manhood and we call on our members to give effect to this resolution'.** The Government responded in July by proscribing Sinn Fein, the Volunteers and the Gaelic League and within days also prohibited the holding of any events or meetings without a permit from the authorities. Central Council called a special meeting on July 30th. The minutes record that O'Toole explained **'the nature of the meeting he had with Dublin Castle whereby he was informed that no hurling or football matches would be allowed in future, whether local or otherwise, unless a permit was obtained'.** The meeting was brief and decisive. Three motions were proposed and passed without dissent:

That no permits be applied for by any Club, Co. Board or Provincial Council and that no member of the Association shall take part in any competition where such a permit may have been procured,
That any person offending against this order becomes automatically and indefinitely suspended,
That all county boards be requested to hold a special meeting within ten days to
> **a, inform clubs of these orders**
> **b, arrange for Sunday ,August 4th at 3pm (old time) a series of matches throughout each county, to be localised as much as possible.**

No doubt the RIC soon became aware of the GAA plan for
August 4th but there was no reaction. This may be because
they either thought it was a bluff or because they thought that
the GAA could not organise and get support for such widespread
defiance and that the occasion would end in embarrassment for
the Association. On the Saturday 3rd a notice appeared in the
national evening papers reminding all clubs and county boards
to ensure full co-operation with the events arranged for **'Gaelic
Sunday'**. Such was the name used to refer to that occasion for
decades afterwards. It was hoped that perhaps forty thousand
people would participate in the matches. The day was an over-
whelming success for the Association. While it was difficult to
arrive at anything like precise numbers some estimates indicated
that 1,800 matches were played and that as many as 100,000
players participated. The occasion was a huge boost for the
GAA and indicated the strength of the organisation and the
loyalty that existed towards it in every part of Ireland. Immediately
the games schedule was in full flow again and without interference
from any Government forces.

Various stories survived afterwards regarding specific incidents
that took place in parishes or clubs aimed at outwitting the RIC so
as to make sure the scheduled matches could take place. Because
it is a Kilkenny story I reproduce the following account from
Mullinavat in south Kilkenny, of their efforts to ensure the match
went ahead on Gaelic Sunday.

Peter Foley owned a saw mill in the village of Mullinavat
and his dance hall was the local hurling club headquarters. He
manufactured hurleys for a number of hurling clubs in the area
and sold them for as little as one shilling each. Because of his
allegiance to his local club it was not unusual for him to supply
hurleys free to the club. In accordance with Luke O'Toole's
instructions, the Mullinavat club arranged the match for 3pm
on Gaelic Sunday but the police, in compliance with the Castle
decree, advised club members that it could not take place. The
Club Chairman, in his reply, informed the police sergeant that
the match was going ahead irrespective of their directive. On
receipt of the Chairman's reply the local RIC decided to raid

Peter Foley's saw mill where it was known that approximately one hundred hurleys were stored in order to confiscate them, this effectively would have made it impossible for the hurling match to go ahead. A local woman, who came in a few days a week to the Barracks to clean it, overheard their conversation and their plans for the raid, and on her return home from her cleaning chores that evening called into Peter Foley and explained what she had heard. He hurriedly buried the hurleys in eight feet of sawdust at the rear of the mill and when the police raided the premises the following morning they failed to find a single hurley. Knowing that they had been outwitted the police surrounded the local playing pitch shortly before the game was due to start but this plan also misfired as the match had been quietly transferred to a pitch some two miles away and took place without any interference or disruption. The Mullinavat hurling club was indeed indebted to Mary Mackey for her neat little bit of intelligence work which caused a very embarrassing weekend for the local RIC unit. (O'Toole, pps. 109/110.)

Towards the end of the year sporting life and life in general was greatly interrupted by the outbreak of the **'Great Flu'**. The epidemic reached its peak about November and caused great distress for many families nationwide. Numerous deaths were recorded, from all age groups, and many well known players succumbed to the disease.

CHAPTER 32

Prospects were much brighter coming into 1919 as the flu outbreak was abating and political upheaval was subsiding. GAA activity re-commenced with great fervour. The Kilkenny county convention was held on February 23rd at City Hall. Sean Gibbons was re-elected Chairman and Michael Moore was elected Secretary, a position he was to retain until 1932. James Nowlan was elected a Trustee along with Michael Moore and Danny O'Connell.

At the annual Congress held on April 20th Alderman Nowlan was again elected President; Harry Boland had been nominated for the position but withdrew his name. A long debate took place on **'the oath of allegiance controversy'**. Civil Servants were obliged to take an oath of allegiance to the British Monarch. This matter had been problematic for some time; it had been debated at a number of county board meetings and in December 1918 Central Council had passed a motion that **'it is incompatible with the principles of the Association for any member to take the oath of allegiance, and any member having done so is hereby relieved of membership pending next All-Ireland Convention'**.

There were very strongly held opinions on both sides as to whether or not such members should be suspended. A motion for re-instatement was lost by 50 votes to 31 with **'the Central Council's decision debarring Civil Servants being upheld'**.

In January 1919 the Central Council took the decision to send a deputation to the **'National Aid Committee'** requesting that some of the funds originally intended for Prisoners Dependants (to which the Association had contributed £700) be **'devoted to those Civil Servants (male and female) who refused to take the oath of allegiance'**. They also decided to run an inter-provincial tournament with the funds devoted to the same cause. Congress also agreed on that occasion on a development programme for Croke Park, this to commence after the All-Ireland finals were played.

The Provincial and All-Ireland championships progressed without interruption from any source. Cork and Dublin qualified for the hurling final which was played on September 21st and resulted in a big win for Cork. It was the first occasion when Cork wore red jerseys. The football final was played the following Sunday. Galway were hot favourites playing against an inexperienced Kildare team. Previous form did not count for much however as Kildare ran out easy winners, 2-5 to 0-1. Both matches drew big attendances; it was estimated that jointly in excess of 55,000 patrons saw the matches. In Kilkenny the deferred 1918 hurling final between Mooncoin and Tullaroan took place on June 29th and ended all square, 4-1 each. The replay saw Mooncoin victorious, 5-2 to 2-3.

On March 11th 1919 a high profile political gathering took place in Kilkenny. The occasion was the welcome home ceremony for the Mayor, Peter DeLoughry; he had spent ten months in Lincoln jail having been arrested in May 1918, as were many others of the Sinn Fein leadership, for their alleged involvement in a perceived **'German Plot'**. While in jail Deloughry had been elected Mayor and in his absence Alderman Nowlan was acting as deputy Mayor and organised preparations for the homecoming event. He also presided at this celebratory function which took place at the Parade in the presence of what the **'Kilkenny People'** described as **'an enormous gathering'** of politicians, including the newly elected Sinn Fein representatives, W. T. Cosgrave for North Kilkenny and James O'Mara for South Kilkenny, friends of the Mayor and well wishers, from throughout the county and beyond.

In the opening address Alderman Nowlan said:

'Fellow citizens at a special meeting of the Corporation I was appointed to welcome Peter DeLoughry on their behalf and on behalf of the citizens of Kilkenny. As you are all aware he was, ten months ago, whipped away out of the country by the emissaries of King George of England and kept in a British dungeon up to this night. I have also been appointed to place around his neck tonight the chain of his office and to install him Mayor of Kilkenny. The 'People' report continued;

Alderman Nowlan then placed the Mayoral chain around Mr. DeLoughry's neck saying 'I have the greatest possible pleasure in putting on DeLoughry, the felon, the Mayoral chain of the City of Kilkenny'.

The Mayor then gave a rousing speech using both the Irish and English languages in which he thanked all who supported him and the national cause they were pursuing.

On September 12th, the homes of Alderman James Nowlan and Mr. E. T. Keane, Editor of the **'Kilkenny People'**, were searched by the police. In the home of Nowlan a revolver and ammunition was found, while in Keane's house two revolvers and ammunition was found. Both were arrested on Tuesday, September 30th at about 6.30pm and found themselves on the 7.45 train to Cork. They were taken to the jail there for Court Martial under Defence of the Realm Regulations. They were detained until October 8th when they were brought to Victoria Barracks, Cork, by lorry under an escort of soldiers and armed police. Nowlan had grown a beard during his time in detention. Alderman Nowlan was charged **'with having on the 12th of last month, in his possession a seven-chambered revolver and seven cartridges, contrary to the Defence of the Realm Regulations'**. Evidence of the finding of the gun and ammunition was given by Sergeant Haran, RIC Kilkenny who stated that the defendant told him he wanted the revolver for protection as he was in the habit of carrying large sums of money. Nowlan was sentenced to twenty eight days incarceration in Cork jail.

James Nowlan's health was now in decline and he retired from his employment. He moved to Dublin to live with his brother John at Mount Brown in the Thomas St. area of the City. He was thus nearer to the administrative centre of GAA activity, this it appears was the reason for his change of residence.

CHAPTER 33

While political activity was of a benign nature in the beginning
of the year this was far from the case as the year progressed. Dail
Eireann was declared an illegal organisation and Sinn Fein and
the Volunteers were proscribed. The army numbers were greatly
increased to deal with the Volunteers. For their part the Volunteers
adopted a much more combative approach. A key element of their
strategy was attacking and burning of police barracks and the
stately homes of the landlord class. The **'War of Independence'**
was now for real. The conflict grew more violent in the early part
of 1920 which turned out to be an horrific year for our country.
Cork's Lord Mayor, Tomás McCurtain, was shot by agents of the
Government on March 20th 1920 and this lead to greatly increased
violence by both sides in Munster. Burnings and shootings were an
everyday occurrence; the burning of barracks was responded to by
the troops with the burning of creameries.

Terence MacSwiney was elected Lord Mayor of Cork in succession
to Tomás McCurtan. At his inauguration he stated **'this contest is
one of endurance, it is not who can inflict most, but who can suffer
most, who will conquer'.**

Many RIC men retired from the force; they could not support
what was happening to their fellow countrymen. In the Spring
police reinforcements were recruited, namely the infamous **'Black
and Tans'.** They behaved more like independent mercenaries
and appeared to shoot and kill on a whim. In July further
reinforcements of troops arrived in the form of the **'Auxiliaries'**,
they complimented the **'Black and Tans'** using similar tactics.
At this stage there were hundreds of Irish men in British jails for
alleged political involvement. Several went on hunger strike to
highlight the abuses perpetrated on the people. Terence MacSwiney
was one such person. He was arrested on August 12th for
possession of seditious documents, was tried by court-martial and
sentenced to two years in jail. He was taken to Brixton prison and
immediately went on hunger strike. Having persevered with a
very long and painful experience he died on October 25th. Central
Council immediately issued the following statement;

Provincial Councils, County Boards, League and Tournament Committees are hereby requested to make next Sunday, October 31st, a closed date all over Ireland so as to record the sympathy of the Gaelic Athletic Association with the Lady Mayoress of Cork in her great bereavement, our admiration for the Lord Mayor's heroic sacrifice and to mark the Association's protest against the inhuman treatment meted out to the Lord Mayor of Cork by the British Government.

GAA members, lead by the President, demonstrated a striking show of solidarity with the MacSwiney family and with nationalist Ireland by their attendance in many thousands at the funeral in Cork on October 31st.

The Annual Congress on Easter Sunday saw a challenge to Alderman Nowlan for the position of President. There were five nominations for the position but after three withdrawals he was opposed by Dan McCarthy, Dublin, who was then Chairman of the Leinster Council. Nowlan survived the challenge by a single vote, 33 to 32. The meeting examined and approved a schedule of developments to Croke Park including increasing capacity and re-surfacing of the pitch. This work was satisfactorily completed by years end. Two motions were passed which have continued to be GAA policy up to the present;

That in future the term of President and Vice-President would be for three years, that All-Ireland finals henceforth will be played in Croke Park.

County Boards and clubs attempted to get field activity underway early in the year but this was not easy as so many members had their focus on military matters; not surprisingly this became more difficult as the year progressed due to the level of strife, particularly in Munster. Towards the end of the year very little playing field activity was taking place other than occasional tournament or friendly matches. In early November the Tipperary County Board requested Jack Shouldice, Secretary of the Leinster Council, to arrange a match in Croke

Park in the hope, as O'Toole states **'that a sizable crowd would turn up on the day and hence raise funds for the purchase of arms for the Volunteers'**.

The match was duly arranged between Tipperary and Dublin for 2.45pm on November 21st. The events of the day, ever since described as **'Bloody Sunday'** are very well documented and it is not necessary to do so again in any detail. It may be sufficient to refer to the **'taking out'** of the **'Murder Gang'** who were recruited to undermine and eradicate Collins' team. Striking first was of paramount importance for survival and that is what happened in the early hours of November 21st when Collins' men assassinated key members of the British gun squad. It is difficult to be definitive as to the number killed, reputable historians are not in agreement; some put the number at 11, some state 14 and others 15.

Fears of a reprisal were expressed; Michael Collins is reputed to have sent word to Croke Park to call off the match. James Nowlan, Luke O'Toole and Dan McCarthy met and discussed the advisability of allowing the match to go ahead. They eventually decided to do so, on the basis that cancelling it might cause increased suspicion, and therefore increased risk, for GAA members. About 10,000 attended and the match was in progress about ten minutes when large numbers of **'Black and Tans'** entered the stadium and immediately started shooting indiscriminately into the spectators and players. Fourteen people were killed including Michael Hogan, one of the Tipperary players. The Hogan Stand was subsequently named in his honour. Central Council now called off all matches until further notice to avoid risk of further retaliation.

In reflecting on the year De Burca writes:

This was the year when first the Black and Tans and later the Auxiliaries were let loose on the civilian population; the year of the burning of Cork, the sacking of Thurles and the pograms in Belfast; the year of the assignation by Crown forces of Lord Mayor McCurtin of Cork and the death while on hunger strike in a British jail of his successor, Terence MacSwiney.

It was the year of continuous raids, arrests and deportations by the British and of guerrilla warfare (including the destruction of 300 police barracks in two nights); the year of the imposition of Partition through the Government of Ireland Act; the year that witnessed the almost total collapse of the British legal system in Ireland and its replacement by the Dail courts operated by the underground republican regime. For the GAA it was the year of Bloody Sunday.

British Army in Dublin, period 1920-1922

CHAPTER 34

1921 was a special year in our narrative. Alderman Nowlan resigned as National President at that year's Congress having given twenty years of exceptional leadership to the Association.

In the early months of the year despite efforts to get competitions underway there was little progress in many counties; too many of the playing membership were in detention, **'on the run'**, or simply too focused on the national struggle, to devote time to sporting events. Some counties, particularly Dublin, did progress their club championships.

In this first half of the year the guerrilla warfare reached new levels of intensity with confrontations between the competing sides being particularly vicious. The newspapers of the time daily/weekly report details of shootings, bombings, reprisals, arrests, court martials and prosecutions. Ambushing was the favoured mode of attack by the republicans as they had intimate knowledge of the countryside and could target the sites most suitable for attack. In one such battle at Castlecomer, in what became known as the Coolbawn ambush, two young men who were very prominent in their respective GAA clubs and parishes, were killed on Saturday 18th June. Sean Hartley from Glenmore and Nick Mullins from Thomastown had both worn the Kilkenny jersey representing their county in football and hurling respectively. Unfortunately for them, and for many others, the Truce which came into being less than a month later, on July 11th, was too late.

Congress took place on March 27th at Croke Park. Only twenty seven members were in attendance including officers and delegates to hear Alderman James Nowlan declare that he was resigning from the Presidency. He was succeeded by Mr. Dan McCarthy.

The following proposals were then tabled and passed unanimously:

That in future each outgoing President be an ex-officio member of Central Council for one year following the termination of his presidency. The present Chairman, Alderman James Nowlan, to be a permanent ex-officio President with power to vote.

CHAPTER 35

James Nowlan's role as Ex-President was mainly in a representative capacity accompanying the President to formal events or deputising for him. Unfortunately numerous such events were funeral services for former friends or colleagues. One such event was for the funeral of his lifelong friend and staunch colleague Patrick Corcoran. They were colleagues in arms through the entire national struggle. He later attended the final of a Memorial Hurling Tournament in honour of Patrick Comerford in Kilkenny, on July 13th 1923. He appeared in an informal photograph taken on that occasion and the caption underneath read **'Ex-Alderman James Nowlan the best-loved figure in the GAA'**. Unfortunately his health deteriorated rapidly in the last year of his life despite the best medical aid available. He spent the last weeks of his life at Jervis St. Private Hospital where he died on Monday, June 30th 1924 at the relatively young age of 62.

The **'Freeman's Journal'** published the death notice on the Tuesday;

Nowlan (Kilkenny) – at Jervis St. Private Hospital, Seamus Nowlan, Hon. President, Central Council, Gaelic Athletic Association (late of Bishop's Hill, Kilkenny). R. I. P. Remains will be removed from Jervis St. Hospital this Tuesday evening at 8pm to St. James' Parish Church. Funeral on to-morrow, Wednesday, to Glasnevin Cemetery after 10 o'clock Mass.

Apart from family and family friends there was an enormous congregation of mourners from all parts of the country representing every unit of the GAA; also present were representatives of Government, all shades of politics in Parliament, local authorities from around the country, also representatives from the Gaelic League, the Trade Unions, the National Army and Industry. His remains were later received at Glasnevin Cemetery by the Chaplan, Rev. Fr. Fitzgibbon. The graveside prayers were recited in Irish by Rev. W. McDonald[26]. In the days and weeks after his death many tributes were paid to him, both verbal and written. I include a selection of written tributes which are still extant and give us a measure of how James Nowlan was assessed by his contemporaries. Senator Peter DeLoughry, Mayor of Kilkenny, received the following message from Mr. W. T. Cosgrave, then President of the Executive Council in Dail Eireann – Prime Minister/Taoiseach;

Government Buildings,
Upper Merrion St.
Dublin.
July 2nd 1924

Dear Senator DeLoughrey, I have learned with a real and personal sorrow of the death of my friend Alderman Seamus Nowlan. In his native city of Kilkenny, which benefited from his labours for a period of considerably more than a quarter of a century, his passing will be keenly felt and deplored, and I am sure that the people of Kilkenny will not easily forget his great services or the inspiration of his noble character.
In the sphere of Gaelic athletics and of the language his loss will be well-nigh irreparable, and we who have intimate knowledge of his endeavours to stimulate interest in our national games and to spread the language of the Gael can appreciate the result in the achievement of which he played such a prominent part.
To the people of Kilkenny and to his afflicted relatives who mourn his loss I offer my deep sympathy. Go ndearaidh Dia trocaire ar a anam.
Mise, le meas,
Liam T. MacCosgair, President.

Kilkenny Corporation met on July 2nd and many tributes were paid by the members. The Mayor then said **'his loss was so great that they felt the Corporation was incomplete without Alderman Nowlan, and almost everyone in Kilkenny felt a sense of personal loss at his death. He might well be described as a man who had grown old in the service of his country; a veteran in the work of Nationality'**. National and provincial newspapers carried reports of his death and in most cases reflected on his career and his work in public life, in the GAA and as a member of Kilkenny Corporation and the many other committees he had served on and supported. I include a tribute from the Nenagh Guardian newspaper on July 5th 1924:

THE PASSING OF A GREAT GAEL
LINK WITH THE FENIANS

The news of the death of 'Jim' Nowlan made many a heavy heart in Gaeldom and filled those of us, his old friends, with a sense of personal loss.

I cannot remember when it was I first met him. He had known me almost before I could lisp. I was a preparatory grade schoolboy when I first began to take notice of the President of the Gaelic Athletic Association. I met him many a time since. I have seen him and been with him at work and at play; in the council chamber; at Gaelic matches almost in every part of Ireland; and when more serious work was to be done. He was always the same quiet 'Jim' – there are few who called him anything else.

He hated prominence. Whenever there was a public function you found him, not seeking the plaudits of the crowd, but doing some humble task, something perhaps that the 'lime-lighters' had ignored as being beneath their dignity.

It was this outstanding characteristic that won him his amazing popularity for there were few more popular men in his or our generations. Witness the actions of the Gaels of Ireland in electing him president of their Association for twenty consecutive years. He loved that Association. Few know how ardently. He was always thinking of it, thinking how best to promote its interests. He gave it out of his best when it was not fashionable to be connected with it. Down through the years he watched its growth and devoted his life to the guiding of its destinies.

It was fitting therefore that the Gaels of Ireland should have bestowed on him the life-Presidency of the Association when with the passing of years the exigencies of the times called for a younger man.

Almost everyone knew Jim in the Gaelic fields. His big-framed figure, his almost boyish genial countenance were familiar everywhere. Anywhere he met you he greeted you in Irish and was ever ready to crack a joke.

Many an hour I spent with him listening to stories of the old Gaelic days, of triumphs and defeats, of the hard up-hill struggles that had to be fought; and now he himself has gone to join the little band that weathered the storms and the furies of prejudice and West-Britonism.

For many years he was senior Alderman of the Corporation of his native Kilkenny and no more popular man ever sat in the Council Chamber in the Tholsel. Slow to enter a discussion, when he did speak one felt that all that one could say was said. He loved the very stones of its ancient walls and when he left it, just a few short years ago, to come to the capital, the parting gave him a bitter wrench.

A member of the Gaelic League since its inception, he was a keen student of the language which he mastered successfully and never lost an opportunity of using it. I remember in the old days when his signature would not be accepted on pay-sheets or advice notes because it was in Irish, he never signed in English.

The son of a Fenian – it was his father who helped James Stephens escape from Kilkenny – he was always prominently identified with the national cause. In the recent struggle he got his share of attention from the British and had been arrested and interned. He supported Mr. Cosgrave at his election in Kilkenny in 1917 and was one of four or five present at the meeting at which Mr. Cosgrave's name was first mentioned as a candidate.

There was another side to his life which few but his most intimate friends were familiar – the domestic side. He had never married, for after the early deaths of a brother and sister, both of whom left orphaned children, he took on himself the care and responsibility of their upbringing. That was the self-sacrifice which was typical of the man. He was extremely generous.

The following letter was published in the Kilkenny people on July 12 1924;

London N 15
7th July 1924

Dear Sir,
I should like to be associated with your expression of regret at the death of the late James Nowlan recorded in your last issue, and it is obvious that the GAA has lost a 'parent' in every sense of the word.
I distinctly remember when in 1896-99, I had on many occasions to discuss GAA matters with him in conference, he was always willing and anxious to impart to those of us who belonged to the younger school of thought the value of his experienced powers of organisation and indeed we invariably felt, even in those days, he was the controlling link in keeping together the Association so far as Kilkenny was concerned.
There were, on occasions, acute differences but Mr. Nowlan seemed to be the outstanding power who realised more than others the value of compromise and his opinions consequently commanded respect and invariably smoothed the troubled waters.
The country delegates, of which I happened to be one, always felt that in Jim Nowlan we had a friend whose advice we could rely on and whose rulings were impartial in a fine point. He was one of the men who appealed to me in those days as the finest type of Gael one could have the pleasure of associating with, a view which I am sure will be reiterated by others who have not seen him for many years but have not forgotten him.
There are men who impress. In justice to Jim Nowlan he was one such.
Yours faithfully,
J.J. TOBIN.

CHAPTER 36

Soon after his death plans for an appropriate memorial to him
were being discussed. Various opinions were canvassed and
many ideas presented but it soon became clear that a playing field
named in his honour was the most widely supported idea. This
solution of course also coincided with the strongly felt long term
ambition of the Kilkenny Co. Board to have grounds of their own,
within the City confines, for the games.

For the record I now document the history of pitch usage by the
County Committee for their important matches, both inter-club
and inter-county, up to the 1920s. The Freshford Road grounds
have already been referred to as a venue for games; the first county
final, in 1887, was played there. Pitches at Larchfield, Palmerstown
and Kilcreene were also used. The All-Ireland football final of 1902
between Dublin and Tipperary was played in Larchfield. The 1905
hurling final between Erins Own (City) and Tullaroan, took place in
St. James' Park on June 3rd 1906. This was the first recorded
occasion when the venue was used by the Co. Board.

The Kilkenny Agricultural Society, which was formed in the
previous decade, had acquired St. James' Park for their annual
shows and other such events. Parts of the lands were laid out as
Hockey and Cricket Grounds. The GAA county committee now
rented the grounds for hurling and football matches and the Park
became the principal venue particularly for county finals and
inter-county matches for the next twenty years.

It turned out that relationships between the Co. Board and the
landlord, the Agricultural Society, was for most of the period a
fraught one. Disputes about rates of rent and property damage
occurred regularly. It appears that for a few years from 1906 they
worked in harmony, reports of GAA meetings in the local media
did not indicate otherwise, but by 1910 disputes and tensions
were commonplace. Reports of county board meetings carried
in the newspapers show frustration by Board members at their
inability to negotiate what they considered reasonable rents. At
the July meeting the Secretary stated they were considering acquiring a
field opposite St. James' Park for their use. Obviously nothing came of
this idea as we find the Mayor in April 1911 attempting to bring

the sides together having arranged a meeting for Easter Saturday in the hope of reaching a mutually acceptable solution. A report of that meeting was heard at a meeting of the Society on April 29th at which it became evident that the Society members believed that the Co Committee were making large profits from inter-county matches played there and hence their desire to get some of the **'cream'**. Further joint meetings clarified that the board got only £30 from the Leinster or Central Councils irrespective of the size of the **'gate'** and in the event of the takings being less than the rent and other expenses the Board had to make up the difference from their funds. Compromise was not reached as we find the Co. Board taking a big match to Waterford in August of that year.

The 1911 series of matches between the visiting American exiles and some of the strongest hurling teams in Ireland has already been referred to. The match between Kilkenny and the Exiles was intended to be played in St. James' Park but agreement was not reached with the Society on the rental question. The County Board then sought and got agreement to play the match in Waterford. The Railway Company put on several **'special'** trains from all parts of the South and brought thousands of spectators to the match – both Kilkenny businesses and the Agricultural Society lost considerable revenue.

The Kilkenny People reports the presence of Alderman Nowlan helping at the entrance gates on that occasion– **'Alderman James Nowlan, the genial President of the Association, was kept very busy. He was beaming with smiles, he always is, but especially when he is kept busy with the tickets – and on all sides he gave his 'Dia dhuit' or 'conus tá tú' to the patrons, most of whom he seemed to know'**. Kilkenny won what was described as a most entertaining match – 4-3 to 2-2.

In 1920 we still find accounts of the same tensions between the parties when the annual rents are being discussed. Reports show that Alderman Nowlan was central to the negotiating sessions during all those years and was time and again on deputations representing the Board.

Due to non-availability of a suitable site, or lack of funds, the Board was dependent on St. James' Park until Nowlan Park became a reality.

CHAPTER 37

It was not until the Spring of 1927 that we find definite progress on the pitch purchase project. The Co. Board appointed a sub-committee to expedite the search for a suitable site. The members of the sub-committee were; Mr. Tom Walsh, Chairman of the Board, Messrs Holohan, Davin, Heffernan, Joyce, Roberts, Butler and Gibbons. (O'Neill, Phil). Progress was rapid from this point and in June the Board announced that land had been purchased from Mr. Peter Corcoran, a local businessman. It is likely that an approach had been made to Mr. Corcoran prior to the appointment of the sub-committee. Mr. Corcoran was the proprietor of licensed premises in John St. where Shem Lalor's is now and had other business interests in town. The agreed purchase price was £700. The Board then agreed to put a levy of £1 on each affiliated club in the county.

About this time O'Neill records **'that President Cosgrave has sent a generous subscription towards the purchase and equipping of the new facility'**. The Leinster Convention held on March 27th allocated grants for the purchase of playing fields including £200 to Kilkenny Co. Board – obviously the project was well underway at this time. At the 1928 Convention the Leinster Council granted a loan of £200 for the same purpose.

June 17th 1928 marked an historic occasion for the GAA in Kilkenny as on that day the first matches were played in Nowlan Memorial Park; the replay of the 1927 Junior Football Championship final between Cotterstown and Conahy acted as curtain raiser for the final of the 1927 Senior Hurling Championship between Mooncoin and Dicksboro. Cotterstown and Mooncoin were the respective winners. The reporter from the **'Kilkenny People'** included the following introductory piece to his report and analysis of the matches;

Sunday dawned on a new era in the Gaelic activities of Kilkenny, when the senior county hurling final fittingly and characteristically marked the opening of our new Gaelic grounds – the Nowlan Memorial Park. The carefully nurtured project, the long cherished ambition, so near and so dear to the heart of Kilkenny's prominent Gaels has at long last

materialised and now we possess a ground for Gaelic games alone; without undue optimism, we can assert that in time it will rank among the leading grounds in Ireland, only surpassed by Croke Park.

Many obstacles have stood in the path of achievement; various contingencies have arisen to retard its progress, but unswerving purpose and resolution, combined with unflagging energy, and enthusiastic Gaelic spirit, have triumphantly surmounted all obstacles and now there stands in the Marble City a glowing tribute to the work of Kilkenny's Gaels and a fitting memorial to one of Ireland's most ardent workers for Gaelic interests, one who was an outstanding figure in the history of the Gaelic Athletic Association –the late Alderman James Nowlan. The new park is yet in its infancy, but even its present crudeness cannot hide the fact that it embodies all the qualities desirable for a Gaelic pitch, and this will become strikingly evident at a later period when the grounds have undergone various adaptations and improvements. The massive concrete entrance ornamented and embellished is singularly impressive and the several automatic turnstiles remind one of the Park in the Metropolis. The seven acre ground is surrounded by a ten foot solid concrete wall. The pitch itself is surrounded by an upright paling and barbed wire after the manner of Croke Park, and the entrance to the enclosure, where its temporary uncovered stand has been erected, and to the sideline seats, is also by means of an automatic turnstile. Every precaution has been taken to prevent the spectators gaining access to and invading the playing pitch, an incident that so often occurred in James' Park with unpleasant results. There is a raised embankment all round, which is a decided advantage to the spectators. The pitch itself is good, but it will take a lot of improvement, spread over several years, before it can really be called an ideal one.

Dan McEvoy remembers the ornate entrance referred to above. He recalls that it was in the form of an arch with crossed hurleys over its centre. He further recollects how it was damaged by a lorry and had to be dismantled for safety reasons. The accident happened in 1947/48 when stone was being conveyed by lorries for the building of the embankment surrounding the pitch from the ruin of the old Kilkenny jail; having tipped its load a lorry was been driven out through the entrance before the lorry body had dropped to its base, the raised body struck the arch causing it mortal damage. The reaction of Paddy Grace, the long-time County Secretary, is not on record!

The official opening of the Park took place on Sunday, August 25th, 1928 when Cork and Dublin met in an All-Ireland hurling semi-final. Prior to the match the grounds were formally opened by Mr. Sean Ryan, President of the GAA. In attendance was the Mayor, Alderman John Magennis, the members of the Corporation, Most Rev. Dr. Collier, Bishop of Ossory, a large number of clergy, and GAA representatives from all over Ireland.

Mr. Ryan in the course of his address said:

"They were dedicating this Park to one of the finest Gaels they ever had in this country, and each and every one of them knew that he was the staunchest Gael that ever left Kilkenny. He played a big part in the administration of the Association for a long number of years. The late Alderman Nowlan was a straightforward, honest Gael. (May God rest his soul). This Park would be a living monument to his work for the Association and to the strong position in which it was today."

The Bishop then blessed the field and expressed the hope:

**"That this field for many long years will be the scene of clean, manly, Irish games, and that commercialism and professionalism, which would ruin games, will be absent from the games played in this park. I can bear willing testimony to the good catholic spirit that has animated all the officials and playing men of the GAA up to this.
I bless this field and hope that for many years the games played on it will be played for the honour of God and for the honour of the fair name of Ireland."**

Many improvements and much upgrading has been carried

out almost annually down through the years. With its excellent playing surface, its extensive seating capacity, its first class facilities for players in the changing rooms, first aid rooms and gymnasium, the Park is now one of the finest and best equipped in the country. It is indeed a fitting tribute to James Nowlan, whose name it bears, and to the entire GAA community in the county.

In June 1926 an enlarged oil painting in a gilt frame of the late Alderman James Nowlan was presented to Kilkenny Corporation by Alderman Peter Deloughry. It has since then occupied a prominent position in the Assembly Room in the City Hall. An inscription attached to the frame records that the subject of the portrait was an Alderman of Kilkenny Corporation from 1899 to 1920. The painting was the work of Messrs Fox, Greenhough and Co.

The plaque reads

Ald. James Nowlan
Alderman Kilkenny Corporation 1899 to 1920

Presented to the City Hall by Ald. P. DeLoughry

CHAPTER 38

The foregoing indicates the close links between the Gaelic Athletic Association and the struggle for national recognition and Independence from its formation in 1884 up to 1921. Responding to strong leadership the members of the GAA bought into the idea of separation from Britain and Independence. The Association acted as a vast network for Nationalists to communicate at local and national level, conveying messages, organising events and supporting one another, sometimes financially. All the above did much to strengthen resolve and promote confidence in great numbers of people to continue the sometimes very difficult campaign. As pointed out earlier a number of the executed leaders of the 1916 Rising were **'GAA men'**.

The Association was central to the resistance movement during the Black and Tan war as evidenced in the difficulties experienced in running the championships at the time due to the participation of so many members in the conflict. The horrific assault on the players and spectators in Croke Park on Bloody Sunday indicated the belief of the Army authorities that the earlier attack that day on their espionage network was carried out by fellow travellers of the GAA membership. Commenting on that event Burke, p. 118, stated;

'This time, unlike 1916, there was no Central Council deliberation, no protest to the British, no contact whatever with Dublin Castle. The GAA was justly proud of the recognition by the British, implicit in the selection of the target for the reprisal, of the Association's identity with what one of the shrewdest contemporary observers called 'the underground nation'.

Is the GAA unique in world history as being the only sporting organisation to be so intrinsically linked with the struggle for the independence of a nation?

I leave that judgement to international commentators/ historians for their assessment!

CHAPTER 39

In the absence of a memoir or personal or family letters we are
dependent on written commentaries by contemporaries in assessing
the personal characteristics and contribution of James Nowlan. It
is helpful that as a high profile person in public life for two decades
many occasions arose when his actions, observations or responses,
were noted and are very helpful in revealing much about the kind
of person he was and about his deeply held beliefs. The Alderman
was a man of large stature and comes across as having a friendly
disposition. He liked meeting and greeting people, made friends
easily and maintained friendships, often despite serious differences
of opinion on matters about which he held deeply felt convictions.
He was big hearted, kind and generous and ever ready **'to get his
hands dirty'** when he saw that a job had to be done.

Due to his lifelong support, encouragement and enthusiasm
for traditional Irish sporting past-times and for the Irish language
James Nowlan can be included amongst the membership of that
body of people loosely referred to as the **Gaelic Revivalist
Movement** which pioneered that patriotic philosophy in the
latter years of the 19th and early years of the 20th century.
Cusack in the Gaelic Athletic Association and Hyde in the
Gaelic League are acknowledged as the principal progenitors of
those respective organisations whose aim was , in the words
of Hyde in a paper read to the Dublin Literary Society on
November 25th 1892, **'to de-anglicise Ireland'**. Their urgings
were responded to by many idealistic people, amongst them poets,
scholars, journalists, Irish language enthusiasts and thousands of
athletes, hurlers and Gaelic footballers. Nowlan was highly supportive
of the ideology enunciated by the **Movement** and was to the fore in
articulating it in local clubs and organisations in Kilkenny City from
the early 1890s.

As indicated earlier in this study Nowlan was from childhood
exposed to Fenian politics and held membership of the I.R.B. as
evidenced in his giving of the Fenian oath to Billy Oates (from
the Waterbarrack area of the City) who related to Jim Maher
'Alderman James Nowlan asked me to join the I.R.B. I took

the oath in the brewery from Pat Corcoran and James Nowlan'.
Later he was an admirer of Parnell and Home Rule politics and
then when Home Rule was not being delivered, he like many of his
contemporaries, supported the Volunteers and the separatist movement.
After 1916 he was very strongly in support of Sinn Féin.

The above political alignments might be interpreted as exposing
inconsistencies in his convictions. In my opinion this would be
totally erroneous and would grievously underestimate his integrity
as throughout his adult life he was entirely motivated in his support of
what was best for his country and for the Gaelic Athletic Association.

It is understandable that during the long Presidency of Alderman
Nowlan the Association was confronted by many controversies,
which sometimes caused serious disagreements or indeed, more
than once, threatened a schism in the organisation. Such fracturing
rarely happened and when it did, as in the case with the Limerick
Board in 1911, reconciliation and healing was soon achieved. It is
reasonable to conclude, in keeping with his general personal traits,
that the President played a key role in the resolution of such
conflicts or orchestrated a situation which brought it about.

Bearing in mind that throughout the 1910 – 1920 period men
such as Harry Boland, JJ Walsh of Cork and many others were most
vociferous in their condemnation of and intolerance of Government
policies and Government representatives; it required level headed
leadership with a calming influence to keep the Association from
adopting a totally political stance which would have been to the
detriment of all members in that period of martial law, curfews,
regular arrests and internments. As President, James Nowlan must
be given credit for leading the Association through that prolonged
turbulent period without compromising its aims or its rules.

People of senior years, such as I, have some awareness of the
contributions of Presidents and General Secretaries/Directors
General to the development of the Association down through the
decades. It is notable that by and large each era produced leaders
of exceptional ability to deal with the challenges facing the Association
in their time.

In my opinion Alderman James Nowlan was such a leader.

References

1 The brewery may have been established as early as 1702.
   See articles by Smithwick and Halpin.

2 Joseph Denieffe, a fellow Kilkenny City man, was born in 1833.
   He played an active roll in the Fenian movement both in
   Ireland and in the USA and was present at the meeting on
   St. Patrick's Day 1858 when Stephens founded a secret
   society which was some years later to become The 'Irish
   Republican Brotherhood' (IRB). It became commonly known
   as the Fenians. He wrote 'A Personal Narrative of the Irish
   Revolutionary Brotherhood', which was first published in
   serial form in the New York monthly 'The Gael' from May to
   October 1904 and subsequently in book form.

3 Denieffe, p. vi.

4 The number of coopers employed in the city fell from 76 in
   1831 to 49 in 1841, source, Neely.

5 Moody, p.108,

6 ibid.

7 Puirsail, p. 34,

8 Cronin, Duncan and Rouse, p. 144

9 De Burca, The GAA, A History, p. 23.

10 ibid., p. 26

11 In January 1887 a Dublin republican group formed to
   organise celebrations to commemorate the 1798 rebellion.
   They became known as the City Hall Committee because they
   held their meetings in Dublin City Hall.

12 Alderman is a very old title referring to members of municipal councils. In James Nowlan's time the first three members elected in a ward (electoral area), male or female, were entitled to use the term Alderman. The Local Government Act of 2001 abolished the title, all elected representatives are now referred to as councillors – no more Aldermen!

13 Walter was from Wexford town where he was born in 1867. He was a printer by trade and having early in his career worked with the 'Wexford People' newspaper he later set up his own printing company. He was for a time secretary of the Wexford Co. Board before being elected as the first secretary of the new Leinster Council. In 1928 Martin O'Neill, then Secretary of the Leinster Council, presented a cup to the Council to commemorate Walter's contribution to the Association. It is known as the Hanrahan Cup and is presented annually to the winners of the Leinster minor hurling championship.

14 Thomas O'Sullivan, Listowel, Co. Kerry, was a journalist and very active member of the Association. Over a period he filled many important positions in his home county and nationally. He was Secretary of Kerry Co. Board, President of Munster Council, was Vice-President and Trustee of the Association.

15 The ground floor now accommodates a Foodhall, part of the Londis chain.

16 Tomás McDonagh was one of the signatories of the Proclamation, he was executed in Kilmainham, May 3rd 1916. He was a poet, playwright and academic. He was on the teaching staff of St. Kieran's College, Kilkenny from the Autumn of 1901 to the Summer of 1903 when he left Kilkenny. He returned to Kilkenny on numerous occasions and remained friendly with James Nowlan despite their differences on the occasion outlined above. McDonagh station, the rail station in Kikenny, is dedicated to his memory.

17 P.D.Mehigan (1884 – 1965) was a sports writer who used the pen name 'Carbery' or 'Pat O'. He was a native of Cork

and covered many sports including GAA, coursing and athletics. He wrote for the 'Irish Times', the 'Cork Weekly Examiner' and several journals and periodicals.

18 For an excellent description of this splendid trophy see Curry in 'Old Kilkenny Review' 1995, No. 47.

19 ibid., Curry pays a fine tribute to Corcoran. The extent to which his life and that of James Nowlan were in parallel is remarkable.

20 For an analysis of nationalism see Cronin, Sport and Nationalism in Ireland,

21 As stated in his Witness Statement Willie Walsh was a Water ford City man. During a long administrative career in the GAA he held many positions of responsibility.   He was, over time, Chairman of the Waterford Co. Board, Waterford representative on the Munster Council and Central Council. He was Chairman of the Waterford Sportsfield Committee and is credited with being mainly responsible for the procurement of the property as an exclusively GAA venue. He was also a prominent referee and over a very long refereeing career took charge of seven All-Ireland finals. The Witness Statement outlines how he spent Easter week 1916 in the company of James Nowlan in Dublin. It is a remarkable coincidence that history subsequently dictated that the County Grounds in Kilkenny and Waterford were named as memorials to those two friends, Nowlan Memorial Park and Walsh Memorial Park.

22 The Bureau of Military history was established by the Minister for Defence and former Officer Commanding Dublin Brigade IRA, Mr. Oscar Traynor, T.D. on January 1st 1947. The objective being **'to assemble and co-ordinate material to form the basis for the compilation of the history of the movement for Independence from the formation of the Irish Volunteers on 25 November 1913 and the signing of the truce July 11 1921'.**

23 **Head Centre**: the IRB membership was organised into what were called **'circles'**. When a member of suitable character was recruited he was called an **'A'** or colonel or **'head centre'**. He then recruited nine **'Bs'** or captains, each captain recruited nine **'Cs'** called sergeants and each sergeant recruited nine **'Ds'** or privates. Thus each **'circle'** comprised 820 members in total.

24 The above is from Witness Statement of Thomas Treacy, Dean St., Kilkenny. He was also incarcerated in Wakefield Prison, being taken there on June 2nd 1916.

25 Tommy Moore was born and grew up in Ballyragget, Co. Kilkenny. He moved to Dublin at an early age, worked in the bar trade and in due course acquired his own licensed premises in the Capital. He had a very successful GAA career both as a player with Dublin and as an administrator. The All-Ireland Senior Hurling Club trophy is named in his memory – the Tommy Moore Cup. For a good representation of his career see Kelleher, and also Nolan. Tommy's love of hurling and enthusiasm for the GAA has surfaced again, this time back in his native Kilkenny. Two of his grandsons, Mícheál and Bríain Ryan are prominent personalities in the Kilkenny GAA family. Mícheál has held the positions of Chairman and Secretary of the Fenians Club in Johnstown. Bríain has won All-Ireland hurling medals at Minor, U 21 and Senior level with Kilkenny. However it is as an administrator that he has made a most significant contribution to the county. He is **'Games Manager'** for Kilkenny Co. Board and in that position is central to everything that happens relating to the games in the county. Tommy Moore would surely be proud.

26 Fr. McDonald was a fellow Kilkenny man. He was a native of Emil, Mooncoin and was steeped in the hurling tradition. He was a priest of the Dublin Archdiocese and was fluent in the Irish language. At that time he was a curate in Fairview Parish, having served in various other parishes he finished

his ministry back in Fairview as Parish Priest. His brother, Mark, played on goals for Kilkenny in the 1920s. He was on the All-Ireland winning team of 1922.

Tommy Moore

Willie Walsh

Bob O'Keeffe, president 1935 - 1938

Luke O'Toole, 1873 - 1929

The Coopers Craft

The craft of **'coopering'** involves the manufacture of wooden casks. Various hand tools were used with great skill to fashion wooden **'staves'** (long thin curved individual sections) which were then fastened together with metal hoops forming different sizes of cask, or wooden vessels such as pails and churns. Coopering has been practiced for many centuries and is still practiced in some parts of the world today. Those who make the casks are known as **'Coopers'**. There are three main categories of coopering known as white, dry and wet. White coopering involves the manufacture of pails, butter churns, tubs and other household utensils for daily use. Dry coopering involves the manufacture of casks for holding dry goods such as flour, tobacco or vegetables. Wet coopering involves the manufacture of casks for holding liquids, it was considered the most highly skilled.

The wooden casks are frequently referred to as **'barrels'** but the word **'barrel'** actually refers to a specific size of cask. Sizes of cask include: Firkin, with 8 gallon capacity, Kilderkin, with 16 gallon capacity, Barrel, with 32 gallon capacity, Hogshead, with 52 gallon capacity, Butt, with 104 gallon capacity.

Different sizes of cask require different sized staves and hoops. The staves and hoops remain in place purely because they are very precisely fashioned. The cooper might have used upwards of thirty different types of tool in making a cask. Coopering demanded great skill and precision. This skill was only learned through a rigorous apprenticeship, which might take from five to seven years. In addition the trade was a 'closed' one so that it was passed down from generation to generation within the same family.

The cooper did not rely on written measurement or patterns to make a cask of specific size. Everything was gauged by the eye and perfection was required since each cask must be airtight, strong enough to withhold the force of fermenting beer, and sufficiently durable to withstand years of rough handling. The coopers were highly paid tradesmen within the brewery.

A cooper could be paid for each cask he made and repaired instead of a weekly wage; this was known as **'piecework'**. Those coopers who could combine speed of workmanship with quality profited handsomely. Coopers on piecework could earn four times as much as a cooper on wages and work lesser hours to do so.

The process of making a cask might involve the use of over thirty different types of tool, mostly used for cutting and paring the wood. Many stages were involved and a cooper might have several casks on the go at once rather than following one through from beginning to end. A brief account is given below of the process outlining the main stages and noting some of the tools used.

Casks were traditionally made using Prime American White Oak. The wood required **'seasoning'** or drying. The timbers for making the **'staves'** were stacked in large piles under cover outside allowing for the free passage of air between them, and were left for a minimum of two years. Then the coopers would carefully select timbers for making the staves and the cask making process could begin.

A cooper first prepared the individual wooden staves, which joined together to form the cask. This stage of preparation was known as **'dressing'**. It involved the use of a variety of sharp paring tools, including an **'axe'** and several differently shaped curved blades. Using these tools a cooper would first cut the stave roughly to size then carefully hone it down to its exact size, and slightly curved shape, using a number of different knives. Then finally the stave was passed over a **'jointer'** (a free-standing plane) angling its edges so it would join smoothly with the other staves when brought together to form a watertight seal. This process would be repeated with each of the staves until there were enough to form a cask.

The staves were then brought together in the next stage known as **'raising up'**. Here staves were gathered and placed standing upright inside a metal hoop forming the cask shape. The cooper then fixed the staves roughly together by hammering a hoop down over their top end. The staves then had to be bent into the characteristic cask shape with tapering ends and a central outward bulge. To bend the staves a special machine known as a **'steam bell'** was used. Shaped like a large bell this machine would be lowered down over the staves and subjected them to high steam pressure which softened the wood.

When the cask was removed from the steam bell coopers would bring together the splayed ends using a rope and then quickly hammer down more temporary hoops over the staves, forcing them to bend together into the curved cask shape. The cask was then placed over a pile of wood shavings which were set alight to char the inside of the cask drying it out, setting its shape and sealing the wood.

The cask ends were then prepared to receive their two lids, known as '**heads**'. Using more paring and cutting tools the two top edges of the cask at either end were cut away into a bevel with the very top edge flattened to ensure the casks would stand steady. Then a groove was cut below the sloping edge with a '**croze**' where the heads would fit. Now the cask was ready for its heads. Before the heads were made and slotted into the grooves at either end of the cask the inside and outside of the cask had to be pared down until very smooth surfaces were achieved. Finally a hole was bored into the side where the wooden bung or cork would fit. This hole was fitted with a brass '**bush**', a brass ring, which lined and reinforced the hole. It was through this '**bung hole**' that the beer could be tapped out.

Now finally the heads could be made and fitted. To make the circular head, comprised of several individual planks slotted together, the cooper used a compass to measure the inside of the top of the cask ends. Then he would cut out the right sized circle, using a '**bow saw**', from the roughly shaped circular head he had made. This was the only time in the whole of the cask making process that a cooper would use such a measuring tool, all other measurements being made with the coopers' skilled and experienced eye. Once cut to shape all the head surfaces were made smooth using specially shaped paring tools, and the edges were bevelled to fit into the thin groove inside the cask ends. Now the two heads were slotted into the grooves at either end of the casks, a piece of '**flag**' (rush) being placed on the inside of the groove first to ensure a watertight seal.

With both heads in place the cooper might make final adjustments by smoothing down the surfaces again and would make a fresh set of hoops, which were hammered down into place over the staves. Finally the heads of the casks were branded with an individual identification number and were ready for use.

(This is an edited extract on the topic from the Guinness website)

Guinness coopers at work

Coopers working, early twentieth century

The world largest barrel producer Guinness

Sources

Beaslai, Piaras, Michael Collins and The Making of a New Ireland.

Coogan, Tim Pat, Michael Collins, Parts 1 & 2.

Courtney, Sean, Purple and Gold, a photographic record of Gaelic games in Wexford, 1885 – 1996.

Cronin, Mike, Duncan, Mark, Rouse, Paul, The GAA, a People's History.

Cronin, Mike, Sport and Nationalism in Ireland.

De Burca, Marcus, The GAA, a History, 1999 and Michael Cusack and the GAA.

Denieffe, Joseph, A Personal Narrative of the Irish Republican Brotherhood

Enright, Michael, Wexford Foundry Disputes, 1890 & 1911.

Foster, R. F., Modern Ireland, 1600 – 1972.

Garvin, Tom, Nationalist Revolutionaries in Ireland, 1858 – 1928.

Halpin, Thomas, 'Themes of Kilkenny's History' – NUI Manooth Lecture Series 1999

Kelleher, Humphrey, GAA Family Silver.

Kilfeather, Sean, Vintage Carbery

Maher, Jim, Kilkenny Through the Centuries.

Moody, T. W., The Fenian Movement (Thomas Davis Lecture Series)

Moore, Cormac, The GAA V Douglas Hyde.

Neely, W. J., Kilkenny – an Urban History, 1391 – 1843

Nolan, William, The Gaelic Athletic Association in Dublin, 1884 – 2000.

O'Ceallaigh, Séamus, The Story of the GAA.

O'Connor, Frank, The Big Fellow.

O'Day, Alan, Irish Home Rule, 1862 – 1921.

O'Neill, Gerry, The Kilkenny GAA Bible

O'Neill, Phil, History of the GAA 1910 – 1930.

O'Riain, Seamus, Maurice Davin, First President of the GAA

O'Sullivan, Billy, 100 Years of Marching, St. Patrick's Brass Band, Kilkenny.

O'Sullivan, Donal J, The Irish Constabularies, 1822 – 1922.

O'Toole, Padraig, The Glory and the Anguish.

Puirseal, Pádraig, The GAA In Its Time.

Ramón, Marta, A Provisional Dictator.

Ryan, Meda, The Day Michael Collins Was Shot.

Smithwick, Peter, K.M., Old Kilkenny Review, 1964.

Post Script

It came to light during 2012 that James Nowlan was buried in an unmarked grave. On being made aware of this situation the Management Committee of Kilkenny Co. Board resolved to have a headstone erected over the grave. Central Council and Leinster Council also enthusiastically supported the project and on July 18th 2013 a simple unveiling ceremony took place. Mr Ned Quinn, Chairman of Kilkenny Co. Board presided. The principal speaker was Mr. Liam O'Neill, President of the GAA.

In a well crafted contribution Mr. O'Neill outlined the pivotal role of James Nowlan in the Association one hundred years ago and the legacy which he and his colleagues passed on. Mr. Padraig Duffy, Director General, was also in attendance as was Mr. Martin Skelly, Chairman of the Leinster Council. The entire officer ship of Kilkenny Co. Board was present. Three generations of the Nowlan family attended and Mr. David Nowlan, Great Grand-nephew of James, spoke on behalf of the family.

The headstone is of Kilkenny limestone. It is adorned by a Celtic cross in which is incorporated the GAA crest. A panel on the face of the pillar displays the crest of Kilkenny Corporation.

The inscription reads as follows:

I mbuan chuimhne ar
Shéumas Ó Nualláin.
(1862 – 1924)

Uachtarán Cumann Luthchleas Gael (1901 – 1921)
Uachtarán Comhairle Laighean (1900 – 1905)
Seanóir ar Bhárdas Cille Chainnigh (1899 – 1919)

A dheartháir Seán, a chailleadh 1946
Agus Bríd, Bean Sheáin, a chailleadh 1940
Atá curtha anseo.

Solas na bhFlaitheas orthu uile.
Ó bhás go críoch – Nach críoch ach athfhás.

On cover flag:

In enduring memory of
James Nowlan
(1862 – 1924)

President of the Gaelic Athletic Association (1901 – 1921)
President of the Leinster Council (1900 – 1905)
Alderman Kilkenny Corporation (1899 – 1919)

His brother John, died 1946
And John's wife, Bridget, died 1940
Who lie buried here.

May Heaven's Light shine on them all.
From Death to Life's end – Not an end but Rebirth.

I mbuan chuimhne ar
Shéumas Ó Nualláin
1862 - 1924
Uachtarán Cumann Luthchleas Gael
1901 - 1921
Uachtarán Comhairle Laighean
1900 - 1905
Seanóir ar Bhárdas Cille Chainnigh
1899 - 1919
A dheartháir
Seán
a chailleadh 1946
Agus **Bríd**
Bean Sheáin
a chailleadh 1940
Atá curtha anseo.
Solas na bhFlaitheas orthu uile.
Ó bhás go críoch - Nach críoch ach athfhás.

Buried with James are his brother John and John's wife Bridget

Maurice Davin, 1842 - 1927

Jeremiah O'Donovan Rossa, 1831 – 1915

Michael Davitt, 1846 - 1906

CENSUS OF IRELAND, 1901.

(Two Examples of the mode of filling up this Table are given on the other side.)

FORM A.

No. on

RETURN of the MEMBERS of this FAMILY and their VISITORS, BOARDERS, SERVANTS, &c., who slept or abode in this House on the night of SUNDAY, the

Number	NAME and SURNAME — Christian Name	Surname	RELATION to Head of Family	RELIGIOUS PROFESSION	EDUCATION	AGE — Years on last Birthday	Months for Infants under one Year	SEX	RANK, PROFESSION, OR OCCUPATION	MARRIAGE	WHERE BORN	IRISH
1	Patrick	Nowlan	Head of Family	Roman Catholic	Read and Write	73		M	Grocer	Widower	Kilkenny City	
2	Ellen	Nowlan	Daughter	R. Catholic	Read and Write	44		F	Seamstress	Not Married	Kilkenny City	Irish
3	James	Nowlan	Son	R. Catholic	Read and Write	36		M	Cooper Journeyman	not married	Co. Kildare	Irish
4	John	Nowlan	Grandson	R. Catholic	Read and Write	10		M	Scholar	not married	Dublin City	Irish
5	Michael	Ryan	Nephew	R. Catholic	Read and Write	5		M	Scholar	not married	Kilkenny City	Irish
6												
7												
8												
9												
10												
11												
12												
13												
14												
15												

1901 Census of Nowlan family

133

CENSUS OF IRELAND, 1911.

Two Examples of the mode of filling up this Table are given on the other side.

FORM A.

No. on

RETURN of the MEMBERS of this FAMILY and their VISITORS, BOARDERS, SERVANTS, &c., who slept or abode in this House on the night of SUNDAY, the and of

NAME AND SURNAME		RELATION to Head of Family.	RELIGIOUS PROFESSION.	EDUCATION.	AGE (last Birthday) and SEX.		RANK, PROFESSION, OR OCCUPATION.	PARTICULARS AS TO MARRIAGE.					WHERE BORN.	IRISH
Christian Name.	Surname.				Ages of Males.	Ages of Females.		Whether "Married," "Widower," "Widow," or "Single."	Completed years the present Marriage has lasted. If less than one year, write "under one."	Total Children born alive.	Children still living.			
1.	2.	3.	4.	5.	6.	7.	8.	9.	10.	11.	12.	13.		
Ellen	Nowlan	Head of Family	Rom Catholic	Read and write		55	—	Single				Kilkenny Eire	
James	Nowlan	Brother	Rom Catholic	Read and write	47		Cooper	Single				Kildare Eire	
Michael	Ryan	Nephew	Rom Catholic	Read and write	16		Scholar	Single				Kilkenny Eire	

1911 Census of Nowlan family

134

SAORSTÁT ÉIREANN.

REGISTRATION OF BIRTHS AND DEATHS IN IRELAND.

Certified Copy of Entry in the Register Book of Births deposited in the Superintendent Registrar's Office.—(See Endorsement.)

1864. BIRTHS Registered in the District of Monasterevan in the Union of Athy in the County of Kildare

No. (1.)	Date and Place of Birth (2)	Name (if any) (3.)	Sex (4.)	Name and Surname and Dwelling-place of Father (5.)	Name and Surname and Maiden Surname of Mother (6.)	Rank or Profession of Father (7.)	Signature, Qualification, and Residence of Informant (8)	When Registered (9.)	Signature of Registrar. (10.)	Baptismal Name, if added after Registration of Birth, and Date. (11.)
44	29th May 1864 Cowpasture	John	Male	Patrick Nowlan Cowpasture	Catherine Nowlan formerly Fitzgerald	Labourer (Cottier)	Anne X Fitzpatrick mark Aurae Monasterevan	4th June 1864	Thomas Carroll Registrar.	

I hereby Certify that the foregoing is a true Copy of the Entry No. 44 in the Register Book of Births of the above District deposited in my Office.

Office, Naas

Date, 25th October 1924

Osopurpal

Superintendent Registrar of Births, Deaths and Marriages,

for the District of Monasterevan

Birth certificate of John Nowlan, James brother in Cowpasture, Co. Kildare

135

Index

Copyright of photographs and images used

Front Cover: David Nowlan   **Back Cover:** Eddie Hughes

Page 1   Parish Church of Sts. Peter and Paul, by Martin Gahan
Page 8   James Stephens, founder of the IRB., unknown & public domain
Page 10   Joseph Denieffe, unknown & public domain
Page 13   Michael Cusack, unknown & public domain
Page 19   Smithwick's brewery, by Martin Gahan
Page 27   Kilkenny City Hall, Courtesy of the National Library of Ireland
Page 28   Bishop's Hill, Kilkenny city, by Martin Gahan
Page 29   Kilkenny Journal & Kilkenny People, illustrations David Nowlan
Page 32   Kilkenny Court House, Kilkenny city, Courtesy of the National
Library of Ireland
Page 35   Alderman James Nowlan 1862-1924, GAA archive
Page 35   Signiture, by Martin Gahan
Page 37   James Stephen's headstone Glasnevin Cemetery, by David Nowlan
Page 41   Poster unknown and photograph, unknown
Page 42   Old Cassidys poster, by Martin Gahan
Page 42   Professor Kevin B Nowlan and Jim Walsh, by David Nowlan
Page 43   Unveiling of headstone, by Jimmy Walsh
Page 44   Kilkenny Volunteers, unknown
Page 45   A Black and Tan, Courtesy of the National Library of Ireland
Page 46   Michael Collins, Courtesy of the National Library of Ireland
Page 47   Mount Brown in Dublin, by David Nowlan
Page 48   Douglas Hyde and Eoin McNeill, Courtesy of the National
Library of Ireland
Page 49   Jeremiah Rossa funeral & Croke Park 1924, GAA archive
Page 51   Luke O'Toole, GAA archive
Page 54   Tomás McDonagh, unknown & public domain
Page 66   Dr. Croke, unknown & public domain
Page 69   The Railway Shield, by Martin Gahan
Page 79   Frank Dineen, unknown & public domain
Page 83   Michael Collins speaking Kilkenny players, (Compliments of Gerry
O'Neill, Dicksboro GAA Club)
Page 102   British Army in Dublin, period 1920-1922, unknown
Page 114   Alderman Kilkenny Corporation 1899 to 1920, by David Nowlan
Page 122   Tommy Moore, Willie Walsh, and Bob O'Keeffe, unknown
Page 126   Guinness coopers at work, unknown
Page 127   Coopers working, largest barrel producer guinness, unknown
Page 129   Headstone, by David Nowlan
Page 131   Headstone close up, by David Nowlan
Page 132   Maurice Davin and Michael Davitt, unknown & public domain
Page 133 & 134   1901 & 1911 Census, courtesy National Archive of Ireland
Page 135   Birth cert of John Nowlan, by David Nowlan

Biographical note re author:

Jim Walsh is a native of The Rower and spent his entire working life in Slieverue – both in Co. Kilkenny.

He has been a life long participant and supporter of GAA activities.

Jim is currently President of Slieverue GAA Club in south Kilkenny. He has occupied every officer ship in the club over the last fifty years including twenty years as Chairman.

He was a teacher at Slieverue Vocational School from which retired as Principal in 1995.

The author wishes to thank Kilkenny Co. Board for the encouragement and support received in bringing this project to publication.